# plus

# 플.러.스.하.다!

박시형, 김태영, 전주영 지음

Talk in ENGLISH+

부산외국어대학교 출판부

Talk in
**English+**

2008년 8월 15일 1판 1쇄 발행
2009년 8월 31일 1판 2쇄 발행
2010년 8월 31일 1판 3쇄 발행

지은이 | 박시형, 김태영, 전주영
발행인 | 유선규
펴낸곳 | 부산외국어대학교

출판등록 | 제 카7-53호 (1988. 9. 1.)
주 소 | 608-738 부산광역시 남구 석포로 15
전 화 | 051)640-3439, 3440 팩스 | 051)640-3580
인터넷 | http://press.pufs.ac.kr
편 집 | 주간 · 서상범, 디자인 · 배영수 · 전지은
인쇄처 | 세종문화사 (051)463-5898
공급처 | 한국출판협동조합 (02)716-5616~9



ISBN 978-89-8312-305-3 93700

값 9,000 원

# 1

## Talk in English+ 들어가는 글

영어를 배우는 사람은 누구나 유창한 발음으로 대화하고 글을 읽기를 원한다. 초등학교에서 시작해서 중학교, 고등학교를 거치면서 영어에 자신감을 가지기 위해 가장 필요한 그러면서도 가장 등한시 되어 온 발음은 국제화 사회를 살고 있는 우리에게 중요한 자리를 차지하게 되었다. 글을 보고 읽을 수는 있지만 알아듣기 쉽지 않은 발음 때문에 혹은 단어와 표현들은 알고 있지만 입으로 직접 소리 내어 말할 수 없는 현실 앞에서, 속으로만 읽고 자신만이 알아들을 수 있는 발음으로는 앞으로 함께 국제화 시대를 살아 가면서 영어를 말하는 사람들과의 원만한 의사소통을 기대하는 것은 무리일 수 있다.

**“발음이 뭐가 그리 중요한가요? 모든 사람들이 각자의 개성에 맞게 영어를 구사하면 되는 것이 아닌가요?”**

라고 물을 수도 있다. 틀린 이야기라고 할 수는 없다. 각자의 개성에 맞는 영어를 구사할 때도 의사소통이 일어 날 수는 있지만 유쾌하고 자연스러운 의사소통이 되지는 않을 것이다. 발음 때문에 무슨 뜻인지 알아 듣지 못해 서로 얼굴을 붉히게 되고 상대방이 자신의 말을 알아듣지 못하거나 오해해서 당황하는 모습에 자신 또한 영어에 대한 두려움과 좌절에 빠지게 되지 않을 것이라 말할 수 없다.

닫혀있던 입을 열어서 소리 내어 말하고 따라 하면서 다른 학생들과 문장을 함께 연습하고 같은 문장들을 반복해서 입에 익히고 책에서 나오는 실용적인 표현들이 나의 것이 될 수 있도록 그리고 내 입이 그 문장들을 기억하고 자연스럽게 나올 수 있도록 하는 것이 영어 발음을 극복하는 방법이다. 마음속으로 단어들을 외우고 문장들을 연습했던 과거의 모습에서, 단어와 문장을 소리 내어 읽으면서 입과 귀와 눈이 동시에 기억하게 하고 자신감 있게 배운 것들을 시험할 수 있는 기회를 가지는 것이 중요하다.

본 교재는 영어 발음에 대한 이해를 돕고 자신감 있는 영어 구사를 목표로 개별 발음의 영역을 넘어서 연음 현상에 대한 연습과 적용, situation을 통한 발음 및 표현 연습과 더불어 다양한 표현

방식과 영어 낱말들을 통해서 반복적으로 연습 훈련할 수 있도록 각 unit 별로 다음과 같이 구성되었다.

### 1. Pronounce it!

각 unit의 처음 부분에 연음에 대한 훈련을 할 수 있도록 몇 가지 표현들과 더불어 target 영역에 대한 이해를 돕기 위해 underline으로 표시하여 연음현상이 일어나는 부분에 대해 보다 쉽게 접근 할 수 있도록 하였다. 이 section을 통해서 학습자는 영어발음의 기본법칙에 대한 지식과 더불어 실제 일어나는 발음에 대한 구체적 발음 방법을 배우게 된다.

### 2. Speak out!

학습자가 위에서 공부한 target 발음 영역이 실제 문장에 적용되어 있다. 이 section에서는 문장 학습과 더불어 앞에서 학습한 발음 영역을 소리 내어 다시 연습하고 문장 내에서 자연스러운 발음이 일어날 수 있도록 연습한다.

### 3. Tips!

위에서 학습한 부분에 대한 이론적 해석을 첨부해서 발음 원리를 좀 더 이해하기를 원하는 학습자가 활용할 수 있도록 한다.

### 4. Situation

24개의 다양한 상황별 dialogue를 엮어서 학생들이 좀 더 흥미를 가지고 발음을 연습 할 수 있도록 할 뿐만 아니라 다양한 영어 표현들을 배울 수 있도록 한다. 이 section을 통해서 학습자는 위에서 학습한 발음뿐 아니라 영어 전반에 걸친 발음, 억양, 감정에 대한 학습을 교육 담당자의 지도하에 할 수 있다.

### 5. Say in English!

앞에서 배운 situation에서 도움이 되는 표현들을 한글로 옮겨 놓아서 수업시간에 학습자가 그 표현들을 익혔는지에 대한 확인 및 평가를 수행할 수 있다. 또한 표현이 간결하여 학습자가 외워서 수업시간에 간단하게 role-play를 할 수도 있다.

### 6. Be brave!

주요 단어나 숙어에 대한 학습을 대화 형태의 문장에서 익힐 수 있다. 학습한 부분이 포함 되어 있는 간단한 대화가 나와 있어서 실생활에서의 단어나 숙어에 대한 활용 영역을 넓힐 수 있다.

### 7. Upgrade it!

주요 단어나 숙어에 대한 학습을 각기 구분된 문장 내에서 익힐 수 있다. 학습한 부분이 포함 되어 있는 각기 구분된 문장들을 학습함으로 단어나 숙어의 활용 영역을 넓힐 수 있다.

### 8. Cultural Tip!

영미 문화에 대한 간략한 소개와 연관되어 있는 여러 가지 영어 표현들을 부담 없이 읽을 수 있다. 이 section을 통해서 기본적인 영미 문화에 대한 이해를 넓힐 수 있다.

### 9. Remember!

각 situation에서 자신이 꼭 기억해야 할 표현들을 적어서 자신만의 문장 사전을 만들 수 있도록 했다. 이 section을 활용해서 학습자는 자신이 필요하다고 생각하는 문장에 대한 학습이 개별적으로 이루어질 수 있다.

### 10. Survive Yourself!

앞에서 배운 situation에 나오는 내용과 응용된 내용을 대화 형식으로 완성할 수 있다. 배운 표현뿐만 아니라 연관되어 있는 다양한 표현과 학습자 스스로가 알고 있는 표현들도 정리할 수 있도록 되어 있다. 이 section을 통해 다양한 상황에서도 대화가 가능할 수 있도록 연습할 수 있다.

위와 같은 학습 구성을 통해서 학습자는 같은 표현들을 다단계에 걸쳐서 학습하게 되고 이를 통해서 발음의 학습 그리고 교정과 더불어 다양한 표현까지 익힐 수 있다. 본 교재 활용을 통해, 실용성이 어느 때보다 중요시 되고 있는 현대 사회에서 "유창한 발음"이라는 날개를 가지고 영어에 도전할 수 있는 멋진 기회가 주어질 것이다.

# CONTENTS

Unit 01

# School Life

# Unit 01

## School Life

### Pronounce it!

Changing Consonants | 이동하는 자음 |

some eggs wash up eat it come on all of tell us
some oranges kiss it an egg has him with us what is

### Speak out!

I need some eggs.

Wash up the clothes.

Just eat it.

All of you should tell us about it.

I have some oranges.

What does it mean?

Put an egg in the bowl.

Is it his or hers?

Believe it or not, he's coming.

Where is everything?

Please stay with us.

He has his own biz with him.

He said he saw it here.

What's he gonna do now?

## Tips!

- 자음으로 끝나고 뒤 단어가 모음으로 시작하는 경우, 이 자음은 뒤 단어의 앞에 옮겨져 발음되어야 자연스러워진다.
- 예를 들어 an orange 에서 앞 단어 an의 끝에 있는 자음 n은 뒤 단어orange의 맨 앞으로 이동한 후 연결되어 발음된다.

## Pronounce it!

Consonant Transfer | 움직이는 자음 |

/w j r l/

which was　kick Roy　job we　big lead　top left

bad legs　help you　love you　move right　make you

## Speak out!

It's bad luck.

I love you.

I'll make you happy.

Which was yours?

This is the job we had.

That's right.

They've left.

What's wrong?

Help with this.

This is half yours.

I'll give you this one.

## Tips!

- 뒤 단어가 자음/w j r l/으로 시작될 경우 앞 단어가 뒤로 이동되어 발음되는 경우도 있다.
- /p, b, t, d, k, g, f, v, (t)s, (d)z, (t)ʃ, (d)ʒ/로 끝나는 단어가 /w j r l/로 시작하는 단어 앞에 오면 이동되어 발음된다.

## Situation 1 Meeting Someone New

Mike: Hi, is this seat taken?

Kevin: Not at all. Were you in Professor Holt's class last semester?

Mike: No, my professor was Ms. Stone.
I'm Mike, by the way. What's your name?

Kevin: Kevin. Nice to meet you, Mike.
Are you also a freshman?

Mike: No, I'm in my second year. Are you from around here?

Kevin: Yes, I grew up here. You?

Mike: I'm from Daegu.

Kevin: Really? I heard that Daegu is famous for its apples.

Mike: It's not only famous for its apples but also women.

Kevin: What do you mean by women?

Mike: People say there are a lot of attractive women in Daegu.

Kevin: Really? I've never heard of that before! I think you could set me up with one of them.

Mike: You must be kidding!

Kevin: Never mind. Anyway, I hope this class is going to be interesting.

Mike: Some of my friends who took this class before said that it was very interesting and worth taking.

Kevin: I'm glad to hear that.

Mike: Let's hope for the best and prepare for the worst just in case.

Kevin: Alright.

## Say in English!

A: 이 자리 비었나요?
B: 아니요.

A: 난 여기서 자랐어요. 당신은요?
B: 전 부산에서 왔어요.

A: 여자는 무엇을 의미하죠?
B: 사람들이 말하길 대구에는 매력적인 여성들이 많다고 해요.

A: 재미있을 거예요. 그런데 혹시 모르니까 최악의 경우를 대비해요.
B: 알겠어요.

## Be brave!

last semester

How many classes did you take last semester?

I took five classes.

professor

Which professor do you prefer?

I prefer Mr. Kim.

second year

Which year are you in?

I'm in my second year.

never mind

What did you say?

Never mind.

worth-ing

Do you think it's worth taking the test?

Of course!

prepare for

How long have you been preparing for the test?

It's been about a year.

study for

Did you study for the exam?

Sure.

just in case

Bring something to eat just in case.

Alright!

## Upgrade it!

professor

He's my professor.

The professor is from Mexico.

My father is a professor.

semester

How many courses do you take this semester?

We offer semester-long study programs in Canada.

I teach one semester a year.

second

What is the second thing to do?

Just give me a second.

On second thought, I don't know why I did that.

famous

He is a famous player.

I want to become famous.

I'm not that famous.

attractive

She looks really attractive.

How attractive she is!

To me, she is the most attractive person in the world.

**never**

I've never done that.

That never occurred to me.

Never say that again.

**interesting**

The novel is really interesting.

He is an interesting person.

Do you want something interesting?

**glad**

I'm glad you are here.

He's glad that his son is safe.

I'm glad to be here.

**prepared**

Are you prepared?

I want to prepare for the test.

Be prepared!

## Cultural Tip!

### 누군가 처음 만날 때

누군가 처음 만날 때 우리가 중학교 시절부터 열심히 외워왔던 Let me introduce myself.라고 말하면 너무 딱딱하다. 개인적으로 몇몇 외국인을 만나거나 자신을 소개하거나 할 때 이제부터는 좀 더 자연스러운 표현으로 자신을 소개하여 딱딱함을 깨뜨려보자. I don't think we've met(만나 뵌 적이 없는 것 같군요)라든지, 실제로 만난 적이 없어도 Haven't we met before? (전에 만난 적이 없나요?)로 소개한다면 정말 자연스럽게 다음 대화로 이어질 수 있을 것이다.

더욱 간단하게 Do I know you?나 Don't I know you? 라고 인사하기도 하는데, 이 표현은 주로 남자들이 마음에 드는 여성에게 접근할 때 쓰는 표현이라고 보면 된다. 혹시나 누군가 나에게 이렇게 물어볼 때, 나도 관심이 있으면 Oh, yeah. 혹은 Sure, well..쯤으로 대답하면 좋겠다. 만약 그다지 관심이 가지 않으면, 간단히 I don't think so. 라고 하면 된다.

**Remember!** Write five expressions of your choice.

1.

2.

3.

4.

5.

## Situation 2 What's up?

**Julie:** Hey Rachel, long time no see.

**Rachel:** Hi Julie. Good to see you. What's up?

**Julie:** Not much. How are you doing?

**Rachel:** Great. Did you do anything special over the vacation?

**Julie:** Just studied for the TOEIC test. How about you?

**Rachel:** I went to Thailand for a couple of weeks.
Have you ever been there?

**Julie:** Yeah, just once. I went there last year.

**Rachel:** You know, I'm thinking about going abroad next year to study English.

**Julie:** Why? There are a lot of places to study here in Korea, for a lot less money.

**Rachel:** Language lessons aren't that cheap in Korea. Plus I've studied English here for years and I still can't speak it well.

**Julie:** Maybe you're not studying right. A lot of people learn English in Korea.

**Rachel:** Yeah, but most of them only study English or have friends from overseas.

**Julie:** True, but you could try and make some new friends.

**Rachel:** I don't want a friend just to use for English practice. That's rude.

**Julie:** Well, it sounds like you have thought a lot about this. Good luck.

## Say in English!

A: 야 Rachel 오랜만이야!

B: 안녕 Julie. 만나서 반가워.

A: 난 태국에 몇 주간 다녀왔어.

B: 나도 작년에 거기 갔었어.

A: 난 내년에 해외에 영어공부 하러 갈 생각이야.

B: 여기 한국에도 공부할 곳이 많이 있잖아.

A: 생각 많이 했나 보구나. 행운을 빌어.

B: 고마워.

## Be Brave!

up

What's up?

Nothing's up.

most of

What do they want?

Most of them want nothing much.

go abroad

Have you been abroad?

No, I haven't.

make friends

Have you made a lot of friends at the new school?

Just a few.

next year

What are you planning to do next year?

I'm planning to get married.

last year

Where did you go last year?

I went to France.

## Upgrade it!

**vacation**

Where are you going on vacation?

Winter vacation is still far away.

During the vacation, we are planning to go to Europe.

**abroad**

I want to go abroad.

Studying abroad is a challenge.

Have you ever been abroad?

**lesson**

You have to learn a lesson.

How was the lesson?

How many piano lessons do you have a week?

**overseas**

I want to go overseas.

Have you ever been overseas?

We need to research overseas markets.

**try**

I tried hard.

Keep trying!

Give it a try!

**practice**

We need more practice.

Practice makes perfect.

You can practice with your partner.

**rude**

How rude it is!

It's not that rude.

He said rude things yesterday.

**thought**

He gave it a lot of thought.

I thought you needed more time.
On second thought, we should do it again.

## Cultural Tip!

**How old are you???**

설마 요즘은 외국인을 처음 만나서 이런 질문을 하는 사람은 없을 것이다. How old are you? Are you married? Do you have children? What is your job? 이런 질문들은 처음 만나 가볍게 하는 질문으로는 곤란하다. 너무 사적인 질문은 기분 나빠질 수도 있다는 사실을 잊지 말자.

**First name? Last name?**

아무리 미국인들이라도 초면에 대뜸 상대방 이름부터 부른다면 다소 불쾌하게 여긴다. 이왕이면 처음에는 Mr. Ms. Miss Mrs.를 붙여 성을 부르도록 하자. 친해지면 자연스럽게 이름을 불러달라고 할 것이다.

**Remember!** Write five expressions of your choice.

1.

2.

3.

4.

5.

## Survive Yourself!

Were you in Professor Kim's class last semester?

Yes, I was.

No, I wasn't. I didn't attend the class.

---

Are you from around here?

Yes, I am.

No, I'm from Daegu.

---

I hope this class is going to be interesting.

I hope so.

Some of my friends said that it wasn't very interesting.

---

How old are you?

I'm 20 years old.

I'm 30.

How old do I look?

---

Where did you come from?

I came from Seoul.

I came from America.

---

Are you also a freshman?

Yes, I am.

No, I'm a sophomore.

---

Unit 02

# Cafe & Restaurant

# Unit 02

# Cafe & Restaurant

## Pronounce it!

t d s sh becomes 김빠지는 /tʃ/ /dʒ/ /ʃ/

/tʃ dʒ ʃ/

that you meet your past you not yet catch you which yard

had your would you change your told you fed your made you

kiss you miss you cash yet walks your fresh yellow business year

## Speak out!

/tʒ

Which yard is better?

She caught you.

Nice to meet you.

I'll paint your picture.

You'd better watch your weight.

I lost your pen.

Let your sister visit your office.

Catch you later.

/dʒ/

Would you like to go?

I fed your dog.

He called your name.

Don't change your mind.

I told you that.

You sold your car?

Don't judge your friends.

Don't feed your dog too much.

/ʃ/

Can I kiss you?

I miss you.

| | |
|---|---|
| I wish you would come. | Did the teacher pass you? |
| Here's the box you needed. | Do you see the difference yet? |
| Wash your hands and face first. | That's a nice dress you're wearing. |

## Tips!

- /t/뒤 /j/음이 오면 함께 /tʃ/로 발음된다.
- /d/뒤 /j/음이 오면 /dʒ/로 발음된다.
- /s ʃ/뒤 /j/음이 오면 /ʃ/로 발음된다.

## Situation 3 At a Cafe

**Cashier1:** Hello, welcome to Starbox. How can I help you?

**Julie:** I'll have a large coffee.

**Cashier1:** Regular or decaf, ma'am?

**Julie:** Decaf, please. How about you, Rachel?

**Rachel:** I'll have the same. Thanks.

**Cashier1:** Would you like anything else?

**Rachel:** No, thanks.

**Cashier1:** That'll be $6.25, please. You can get your drinks over there at the pick-up counter.

**Cashier2:** Two large decafs. Here you go.

**Rachel:** Thank you. Can you get some cream and sugar for me?

**Julie:** Sure.

**Rachel:** Have you seen the Herman Hesse exhibition at Busan Museum?

**Julie:** Yes, I went last weekend. It was fantastic. Mike wants to see it, too. You should go together.

**Rachel:** Great idea. I'll give him a call later.

**Julie:** Anyway, I sense there is something going on between you two.

**Rachel:** What's that supposed to mean? Me and Mike? Oh, no. We are just friends.

**Julie:** Okay, let's see what happens. People say you guys are going out together a lot recently.

**Rachel:** Julie, I'm not going out with him a lot. I mean it. You have my word that there is nothing going on between me and Mike.

**Julie:** Alright, alright. Don't get too serious about it.

**Rachel:** I just don't want to spoil my friendship with him.

**Julie:** I understand. Speaking of friendship, aren't you hanging out with Carol lately? I haven't seen you with her recently. Is there anything wrong?

**Rachel:** Speak of the devil, there is Carol!

## Say in English!

A: 어떻게 도와드릴까요?
B: 커피 큰 것으로 하나 주세요.

A: 크림하고 설탕 좀 가져다 줄래?
B: 응.

A: 부산박물관에서 Herman Hesse 전시회 봤니?
B: 응, 지난 주말에 갔었어.

A: 사람들이 요즘 너희들 같이 자주 다닌다더라.
B: 나 그 애하고 자주 다니지 않아! 정말!

## Be brave!

how about

How about going to the movies together?

That sounds fine.

spoil

Who spoiled him?

His mom did. He's such a mama's boy.

exhibition

Where did you guys meet?

At an exhibition.

go on

What's going on here?

I have no idea. Find out about it yourself.

devil

Why does he act like that?

Maybe he is possessed with a devil!

happen

What happened to you?

I was in an accident.

## Upgrade it!

regular

I usually keep regular hours.

I'm in regular work.

Regular exercise is important for your health.

exhibition

What is the theme of the exhibition?

I went to the exhibition last month.

The exhibition was the greatest.

fantastic

It was fantastic.

That sounds fantastic.

This is the most fantastic show I've ever seen.

sense

That makes sense.

Please use a little sense.

I sense much fear in you.

serious

Don't be too serious.

I'm serious.

There is a serious problem in our robot.

spoil

The cookie spoiled my appetite.

The rain spoiled my holiday.

The heavy rain spoiled the crops.

hang out

Do you hang out with him?

Please hang out the flag.

I don't want to hang out with him anymore.

lately

I haven't seen him lately.

He's been working very hard lately.

What have you been up to lately?

**devil**

Once a devil, always a devil.

She is possessed by a devil.

## Cultural Tip!

In a Restaurant

전 세계 문화가 다른 만큼 식사 문화도 나라마다 아주 다양하다. 우리나라에도 워낙 보편화되어 있어 family restaurant에도 한번쯤 가봤을 것이다. 이제 외국의 음식점에 들어가서 식사한다고 해도 많이 당황스럽지는 않으리라 본다. 외국에서 레스토랑에 들어가면 바로 테이블에 앉는 것이 아니고 일단 직원이 테이블로 안내를 해준다. 그런 다음 메뉴를 보고 주문하면 된다.

Appetizer/ 전채요리는 식사 전 가볍게 입맛을 돋우기 위한 음식이므로 맛있다고 너무 많이 먹어버리면 주 메뉴 음식을 많이 못 먹게 된다.

Entre/ Main Dish는 주 메뉴이며 육류나 해산물 등이 흔히 나온다. 스테이크를 주문하면 How do you like your steak?라고 웨이터가 물어본다. 그럴 땐 Well-done, Medium, Rare 등으로 말하면 된다.

Dessert/ 우리도 식후 가볍게 과일을 먹거나 음료를 마시곤 하는데, 서양사람들의 후식은 과일, 과자, 케이크 등 정말 다양하고 종류도 아주 많다.

외국 레스토랑에서는 식사 후 계산을 테이블에서 하는 것이 일반적이다. Please, bring my check (bill).라고 하면 웨이터나 웨이트리스가 계산서를 들고 친절하게 계산을 도와준다.  물론 tip도 잊으면 곤란하다. 흔히 10~20% 정도가 적당하다고 한다.

**Remember!** Write five expressions of your choice.

1.

2.

3.

4.

5.

## Situation 4 At a Restaurant

**Host:** Good evening.

**Mike:** Mike and Rachel, we have a reservation for 7:00.

**Host:** Yes. Follow me please. Smoking or non-smoking?

**Mike:** Non-smoking please.

**Host:** Will this be alright?

**Mike:** Do you have a table next to the window?

**Host:** How is this?

**Mike:** Much better, thank you.

**Host:** Today's special is rib-eye steak and pasta for $20. Your waiter will be with you shortly.

**Rachel:** Thank you. Everything looks delicious.

**Waiter:** Hello! My name is John. I'll be your waiter this evening.
Can I get you anything to drink?

**Mike:** I'd like lemonade.

**Waiter:** Sure. And for you, ma'am?

**Rachel:** I'll have a glass of red wine.

**Waiter:** Would you like an appetizer?

**Mike:** What do you think, Rachel?

**Rachel:** Let's get this green salad.

**Waiter:** Ok, I'll be right back with your drinks and the salad.

**Mike:** It's been a long time since we came here last time. It's been about a year or so, I guess.

**Rachel:** Yeah, that's a long time. We should come here more often.

**Mike:** I think so, too. Anyhow, we are here to have this great food for ourselves.

**Rachel:** That's right.

**Mike:** So, how's your school life? Is there any fun?

**Rachel:** It's just great. I like what I do there, plus people are friendly.

**Mike:** Good to hear that!

**Waiter:** Here are your drinks and salad. Are you ready to order?

**Rachel:** Yes, I'll have the New York steak.

**Waiter:** How would you like that?

**Rachel:** Medium rare, please.

**Waiter:** Okay. That comes with soup, and potato or sweet potato.

**Rachel:** I'll have the sweet potato, please.

**Waiter:** Thank you, how about you, sir?

**Mike:** What's in your seafood spaghetti?

**Waiter:** Crab, squid, and clams.

**Mike:** Okay, I'll have that with a cup of onion soup.

**Waiter:** Will that be all?

**Mike:** Yes, thank you.

**Waiter:** Okay, call me if you need anything else.

## Say in English!

A: 창문 옆 테이블 있나요?
B: 이 곳은 어때요?

A: 마실 것 좀 가져다 드릴까요?
B: 전 레몬에이드 주세요.

A: 여기 온지 참 오래간만인 것 같아.
B: 응, 오래됐지.

A: 학교생활은 어때? 재미있어?
B: 아주 좋아.

## Be brave!

reservation

I have a reservation for 7:00.
But you didn't confirm it and it was canceled.

shortly

When will he arrive?
He will arrive shortly.

next to

Who's sitting next to her?
That's probably John.

friendly

What's your English teacher like?
She's friendly.

last time

What did you do last time you met each other?
We just had coffee and that's all!

onion

What kind of soup would you like?
Onion soup please.

## Upgrade it!

**reservation**

I need to make a reservation.

We have serious reservations about the project.

Your reservation for the seminar has been accepted.

**special**

You are so special.

You need special treatment.

Is she someone special to you?

**delicious**

It's really delicious.

I had a delicious lunch with him.

The cookies look really delicious.

**appetizer**

Do you want some appetizers?

Enjoy free appetizers!

Appetizers will be served in a moment.

**salad**

Which salad do you want?

The fruit salad is on display.

I'd like the chicken salad.

**sweet**

It's sweet.

How sweet you are!

I like sweet things.

## Cultural Tip!

Slow Food? Fast Food!

외국을 다니다 보면 간단하게 허기를 때울 수 있기에 적당한 곳들이 참으로 많다. 가격도 저렴하고 종류도 다양하다.

Cafeteria/ fast food restaurant/ Self service이다. 그러나 fast food 음식점보다 좀 더 식사 같은 요리를 맛볼 수 있다고 보면 된다. Main dish는 메뉴를 보고 주문하고 salad나 dessert등 side dishes는 직접 진열대에서 골라오면 된다.

Drive-in Restaurant/ 차에 탄 채로 주문하고 차 안에서 식사 가능한 식당이다.

Coffee shop/ 꼭 커피만 마시는 것이 아니라 doughnut, toast, sandwich등을 곁들인 식사도 가능한 곳이다.

Delicatessen/ 큰 Mall이나 department store내의 스낵코너를 말한다. 줄여서 deli라고 한다.

Snack bar/ hamburger, sausage, chicken, salad등과 음료수를 파는 간이 식당이다

| **Remember!** | **Write five expressions of your choice.** |
|---|---|
| 1. | |
| 2. | |
| 3. | |
| 4. | |
| 5. | |

## Survive Yourself!

Would you like anything else?

Yes, please.

No, thanks. I'm full enough.

Nope, that's enough.

Well, just a little bit, then.

You can get your drinks over there at the pick-up counter.

Thanks.

You mean right over there?

I see.

---

I'll give him a call later.

Do you know his number?

But he said it's an urgent call.

Ok.

---

What's that supposed to mean?

It means that you are not as ugly as you think.

It means that you are perfect for the job.

It means that he's not that indifferent to you.

Well, it's nothing. Just forget about it.

---

Don't get too serious about it.

But I can't help thinking about it.

But it's really important to me.

Ok, I'll try not to.

Thanks, anyway.

---

Do you have a table next to the window?

How about this one?

Oh, yes. This way, please.

Of course we do.

Yes, ma'am(sir).

---

Everything looks delicious.

Yes, especially those ones.

Yes, my mouth is watering now.

Hmm.. yummy!

---

We should come here more often.

That's what I'm thinking about.

That's right.

Yes, I like this place.

---

I like what I do there, plus people are friendly.

That sounds good.

Good for you.

Good to hear that.

---

Unit 03

# Movies

Talk in ENGLISH+

# Unit 03

# Movies

## Pronounce it!

**Unreleased Consonants 터지지 않는 /p t k/**

/p t k/

stop that  help that  hope that  wrap this  hit Betty  got fired  hot food  shot for

fat boy  not that  like this  back home  pick this

## Speak out!

Stop that lady!

He got fired.

It's not that.

Pick this up.

I quit playing.

Who hit Betty?

Can I look now?

Wrap this up.

Please wrap this up.

He is a fat boy.

Will you help that lady?

I want some hot food.

We walk fast.

She got fired.

That pen's mine.

Let's quit for a while.

## Tips!

- /p t k/는 원래 터뜨리며 발음하지만 뒤에 다른 자음이 오면 터뜨리며 발음하지 않고 순간적으로 호흡을 멈추듯 발음한다.

## Situation 5 At the movies

Rachel: Which movie do you want to see?

Julie: I heard *Ocean's 15* is great.

Rachel: Hi, two tickets for *Ocean's 15*, please.

Cashier: Ok. For 8:00 or 9:30?

Rachel: Eight O'clock please.

Cashier: Here are your tickets. That will be $16, please.

Rachel: Here it is.

Cashier: Thank you. Enjoy the movie.

Julie: Do you want something to eat?

Rachel: That's a good idea. How about some popcorn?

Julie: That would be nice.

Rachel: Hi, one large popcorn and two medium sodas, please.

Cashier: That'll be $8.

Julie: Who is starring in the movie, anyway?

Rachel: George Clooney, Brad Pitt, Mat Damon, Andy Garcia, and so on, I think.

Julie: Did you see *Ocean's 14*?

Rachel: I've seen all the series.

Julie: That's amazing. Which one was the best?

Rachel: I think the second one was very exciting.

Julie: I think I should rent the DVD.

Rachel: That's your call, but you won't regret it.

## Say in English!

A: 어떤 영화 보고 싶니?

B: Ocean's 15가 재미있다던데.

A: 뭐 좀 먹을래?

B: 좋은 생각이야.

A: 너 Ocean's 14는 봤니?

B: 난 모든 시리즈 다 봤어.

A: DVD로 빌려봐야겠어.

B: 그건 네가 결정할 일이지만 후회하진 않을 거야.

## Be brave!

enjoy

Did you enjoy yourself at the party?

Not really!

amazing

What's so amazing about him?

He got nominated for the Nobel Peace Prize.

rent

My rent is so high.

Move out and get a cheaper house.

regret

Do you regret not having studied hard enough in your school days?

No, I can start anew any time.

want to

What do you want to do right now?

The only thing I want is to go to sleep!

exciting

How was the game?

It was very exciting.

## Upgrade it!

**heard**

I heard that you are new here.

I've heard a lot about you.

**enjoy**

Enjoy your dinner!

They are enjoying their meal.

We enjoyed listening to the music.

**star**

He became a star.

In the movie he stars as Frodo Baggins.

It stars Jennifer Aniston.

**amazing**

It's really amazing.

It would be an amazing adventure.

Another amazing fact, you actually came down here to meet me in person.

**rent**

We rented a car yesterday.

She rents a house with three other girls.

She rented rooms to college students.

**regret**

I regret having spent the money.

He regretted his mistake.

I have nothing to regret.

## Cultural Tip!

Visitor's Center

여행시 돌아다닐 때는 우선 관광안내소(Visitor's Center)부터 들르는 것이 좋다. 이 곳에서 관광지에 대한 안내 책자를 받을 수 있다. 관광지 외에도 놀이공원이나 극장 등에도 갈 수가 있는데 입장권은 그곳에 가서 끊거나 전화로 예약할 수 있다. 미국 영화관은 예매해도 좌석이 open seating, free seating이라고 하여 지정되어 있지 않으므로 먼저 온 사람이 원하는 자리에 마음대로 앉을 수 있다. 그러므로 조금 서둘러 입장하는 것이 좋다.

| **Remember!** | Write five expressions of your choice. |
|---|---|
| 1. | |
| 2. | |
| 3. | |
| 4. | |
| 5. | |

## Situation 6 What's playing?

**Kevin:** Do you want to see a movie tonight?

**Carol:** Hmm. Maybe. What's playing?

**Kevin:** How about the new James Bond film? I heard it's really exciting.

**Carol:** Actually, the last one was rather boring.

**Kevin:** What about the movie based on Stephen King's new novel?

**Carol:** I don't know. His books are usually fascinating, but I don't like horror movies.

**Kevin:** Well, what do you want to see?

**Carol:** I'm interested in the new Halle Berry movie. It looks good.

**Kevin:** Hmm. I personally don't like Halle Berry, but if you insist.

**Carol:** You don't have to. How about the new Japanese animation?

**Kevin:** You mean The Girl Who Leapt Through Time?

**Carol:** Yes, I heard that movie is well-made and it makes us think.

**Kevin:** I don't know what to say. I don't particularly like Japanese movies.

**Carol:** I think we have a problem here. That means you really want to see the James Bond film, and there is no alternative.

**Kevin:** I'm afraid so. Carol. Please. I really want to see the movie, and all my other friends have already seen the movie. I don't want to watch it alone.

**Carol:** Alright, alright, alright. That's enough. Don't grumble about it. Let's see what you want to see today, and next time we watch what I want. Deal?

**Kevin:** Deal! Thanks Carol. You are always so generous and forgiving. I'm so lucky to have a friend like you.

**Carol:** Don't flatter me! Let's go.

## Say in English!

A: 오늘 저녁에 영화 볼까?
B: 음, 아마도. 뭐 하는데?

A: 난 이번에 새로 나온 Halle Berry의 영화에 관심 있어.
B: 음. 난 개인적으로 Halle Berry 별론데.

A: 내가 듣기로 그 영화는 잘 만들어졌고 생각하게 하는 영화라고 하더라.
B: 뭐라 말해야 할지. 난 특히 일본영화 안 좋아하는데.

A: 난 너 같은 친구를 둬서 행운이야.
B: 아부하지 마.

## Be Brave!

fascinating

How was the movie last night?

It was fascinating.

usually

What do you usually do in your free time?

I usually watch TV.

insist

Did he insist that you should pay for it?

Yeah, he's such a stubborn old man.

well-made

How do you like the new movie?

I think it's well-made.

personally

Don't take it personally.

I won't.

grumble

What is he grumbling about?

About everything. He is hard to satisfy.

## Upgrade it!

**rather**

I would rather die than yield.

**fascinating**

It's so fascinating.

She is a fascinating speaker.

It's a fascinating city.

**well-made**

There are several well-made movies recently.

The books are well-made.

It's well-made.

**particularly**

I don't particularly like the movie.

That necklace looks particularly attractive on you.

The homework is particularly important.

**alternative**

No alternative is left.

What alternative do we have?

**grumble**

He grumbles about everything.

She grumbled over the food.

He grumbles at his father all the time.

**generous**

He is so generous.

You are a generous giver.

**forgiving**

He is forgiving.

How forgiving are you?

I'm not very forgiving.

## Cultural Tip!

**영화관 관련 용어**

영화관 관련 여러 용어를 미리 익혀두자. 우리나라처럼 외국에서도 ticket booth에서 표를 구입한다.

Ticket Booth = Box Office 매표소

Adult/ Child 성인/어린이

Year Pass = Annual Pass 연간 입장권

Senior Discount/ Student Discount 연장자 할인/ 학생 할인

Section/ Aisle 구역/ 통로번호

Row/ Box 열/ 칸막이 좌석

Admission Fee 입장료

Restoration Fee 반환 수수료

No Children Under 5 Years 5세 이하 어린이 관람 불가

MAT = Matinee 주간상영(낮에는 30% 정도 저렴하다)

No picture = No camera allowed 사진촬영금지

No Flash 플래시를 터뜨리지 마시오

Presents 배급사

Production 제작사

Produced by 제작

Directed by 감독

Music by 음악

## Remember!

**Write five expressions of your choice.**

1.

2.

3.

4.

5.

## Survive Yourself!

Which movie do you want to see?

How about a Japanese animation?

Well, what about you?

Iron Man, of course!

Do you want something to eat?

That's a good idea.

Yes, how about some popcorn?

Let's have some hotdogs.

Yes, I want something.

Who is starring in the movie?

Tom Cruise is the lead role

Brad Pitt, I guess.

I have no idea.

Well, let's see

I've seen all the series.

How was it?

Did you like it?

Which scene is the most impressive?

Do you want to see a movie tonight?

I don't think so.

Well, I have plans.

Yes, of course.

Hmm, maybe. What's playing?

I heard it's really exciting.

That's what I've heard.

Oh, really?

Well, then. Do you want to recommend it?

I personally don't like Halle Berry, but if you insist.

I don't, either, but the movie is really good.

Oh, no. That's ok. If you are not interested, I don't want to insist that you watch it.

You don't have to.

Don't grumble about it!

Ok, ok. I got it.

No, it's not grumbling or something like that.

Ok, sorry to bother you.

You are always so generous and forgiving.

Thank you for saying so.

Don't flatter me.

That's what YOU are.

Unit 04

# Dating

Talk in ENGLISH+

# Unit 04

# Dating

## Pronounce it!

Glottal Stop 숨막히는 / t /

/ t /

that one  not close  get going  get gas  hot weather  what kind

meet with  put water  cut glass  got clean  but we  fat kid  hit one

## Speak out!

Where do you get gas?

That one is mine.

It's not close.

Let's get going.

Try to hit one.

Do you want to cut glass?

That could help.

It's not worth it.

She went with him.

What kind of gate do you like?

She's a smart woman.

## Tips!

- / t/ 뒤에 /w g k /가 오면 성대 사이의 숨통이 일시적으로 막혀버리며(헉! 헙! 윱! 얼!) 폐쇄되어 숨막히는 발음이 된다. 발음을 빨리 하다 보면 성대가 막히듯 발음될 때도 있는 법이다.
- /r/은 입술을 '우' 하듯이 조금 동그랗게 하고 혀 가운데를 구부려 낸다. 혀 끝이 입천장에 닿지 않도록 주의한다. 입천장에 닿으면 /l/음이 된다.

## Situation 7 Set me up!

Julie: I'd like to have a boyfriend.

Rachel: I can set you up with my best friend. He's interested in meeting someone, too.

Julie: What does he look like?

Rachel: He's kind of tall and very good-looking. He has dark hair and a great smile.

Julie: What's he like?

Rachel: He's charming and has a great sense of humor, but he can be a little stubborn from time to time.

Julie: Sounds like I should give it a try.

Rachel: Of course you should. He's a great guy. Let's say this Saturday. Is it alright?

Julie: Let me check my schedule. Oh, my parents are coming this weekend. I have to be with them all weekend.

Rachel: Oh, then how about next Wednesday after school?

Julie: That sounds fine with me.

Rachel: Alright. Then, I will tell him all the good things about you, and convince him that he should meet you.

Julie: Thanks, but don't brag about me too much.

Rachel: No worries.

## Say in English!

A: 그 사람 어떻게 생겼니?
B: 키 크고 잘 생기고.

A: 성격은?
B: 매력적이고 유머 넘치고.

A: 그러면 다음주 수요일 학교 마치고 어때?
B: 괜찮게 들리는데.

A: 내 자랑 너무 하진 마라.
B: 걱정하지마.

## Be brave!

brag

Did you meet him?

Yeah. He bragged about everything and I was really disappointed.

stubborn

How do you describe your personality?

I am a little stubborn.

parents

Are both of his parents still alive?

No, he has been brought up by a single mom.

sound

How do I sound?

You sound awful.

convince

Can you convince him that you are the perfect match for him?

Of course I can!

kind of

Where do you want me to put it?

It's kind of hard to say.

## Upgrade it!

**interested**

Are you interested in him?

If you are interested, please give us a call.

We invited all the people who were interested.

**charming**

I met a guy who was very charming.

She is charming.

It's not easy to find a Prince Charming.

**sense**

He has no common sense.

It makes plenty of sense.

It makes no sense.

**stubborn**

He is as stubborn as a mule.

In general, they are stubborn rather than cooperative.

You are just being stubborn.

**convince**

It's not easy to convince him.

We convinced her of her error.

I can convince him.

**brag**

He always brags about his rich father.

It's just nothing to brag about.

Don't brag!

## Cultural Tip!

남자나 여자를 묘사할 때 영어로는 묘사하는 단어들이 무척 다양하다. smart는 똑똑하고 재치 있게 말을 잘하는 사람을 뜻한다. fun이라고 하면 '유머감각이 있고 함께 있어 즐거운' 사람을 가리킨다. 미국 사람들도 우리처럼 유머감각이 풍부한 사람을 좋아한다.

여자를 묘사할 때 우리는 흔히 귀엽다는 의미로 cute이라고 하는데 영어로는 '외모가 매력적인' 이라는 뜻을 가진다. 우리가 사용하는 귀엽다는 의미와는 달리 남녀 누구든 외모가 매력적이면 쓸 수 있는 단어다. sweet은 '다정하고 친절한'이라는 의미이다.

| **Remember!** | **Write five expressions of your choice.** |
|---|---|
| 1. | |
| 2. | |
| 3. | |
| 4. | |
| 5. | |

## Situation 8 How did your date go?

Rachel: Tell me about your date last night.

Julie: It was good at first 眀We were having a nice meal at a fine restaurant, when he suddenly realized he forgot to bring his wallet.

Rachel: Oh, no! What did you do?

Julie: He tried to get his roommate to bring his wallet to the restaurant, but his roomie was studying at the library.

Rachel: What happened then?

Julie: I had to wait for about 30 minutes while he went back home to get his wallet.

Rachel: How embarrassing! Didn't you have any money, anyway?

Julie: I did, but he insisted that he should pay.

Rachel: That's ridiculous.

Julie: Anyway, after the dinner, we kind of had some quality time together.

Rachel: What's that supposed to mean? After THAT dinner, you guys went to other places and had fun? I don't get it.

Julie: Other than the dinner incident, he was very nice, kind, and even very funny.

Rachel: Good to hear that.

Julie: Thanks Rachel! You are my best friend.

Rachel: I hope you guys get along well.

## Say in English!

A: 어제 데이트에 대해 한번 말해봐.
B: 처음에는 괜찮았지.

A: 나도 돈이 있었는데 그가 계속 돈 내겠다고 고집부리더라고.
B: 참 이상하네.

A: 저녁식사 사건을 제외하면 그 사람 매력 있고 친절하고 심지어 재미있더라.
B: 그나마 다행이네.

A: 너희들 잘 지내길 바래.
B: 걱정해 줘서 고마워.

## Be brave!

have fun

Did you have fun at the picnic yesterday?

No, we were caught in a shower.

embarrassing

What kind of situation has been the most embarrassing for you?

When I was talking about something and I suddenly realized nobody was listening.

wallet

I forgot where I had put my wallet.

Did you look in your purse?

realize

You don't realize how much I love you.

So what do you want me to do?

pay

How much do I have to pay for this?

Nothing, I'm paying for it.

suddenly

Where did you go last night in the middle of the conversation?

Suddenly I remembered I had forgotten about something.

## Upgrade it!

fine

Fine feathers make fine birds.

That's fine with me.

suddenly

She cried out suddenly.

He was suddenly taken ill.

The car stopped suddenly.

embarrassing

I was in an embarrassing situation.

That's very embarrassing.

It's embarrassing to talk about myself.

insist

He continued to insist that I misled him.

She insisted that the pen was hers.

If you insist on smoking in the restaurant, you will be asked to leave.

ridiculous

You are making a ridiculous claim.

I've never heard anything so ridiculous.

You look ridiculous.

quality

He bought some quality furniture.

They are the best quality you can buy.

I need some quality time.

## Cultural Tip!

Hello? Hello!

우리는 hello를 전화 받을 때 '여보세요' 하거나 인사할 때 '안녕하세요'라고 한다. 그러나 이외에도 hello에는 많은 다양한 뜻이 있다. 어이없을 때, '뭐라고?'라는 의미로도 쓰고, 상대가 눈치채지 못할 때 주의를 환기시키기 위해 쓰기도 한다.

Please? Please!

please도 보통 정중히 말하거나 부탁할 때 쓰는데, 그 외 상대방에게 화가 나거나 놀랐을 때, '웃기고 있군', '말도 안돼!'등의 의미로 쓰이기도 한다.

| **Remember!** | **Write five expressions of your choice.** |
|---|---|
| 1. | |
| 2. | |
| 3. | |
| 4. | |
| 5. | |

## Survive Yourself!

I can set you up with my best friend.

Oh, thank you.

Oh, really? What's he like?

Well. No, thanks.

What does he look like?

He looks attractive.

Well, he is average height with dark hair.

You may guess!

---

Let's say this Saturday. Is it alright?

Sorry, but I have another appointment.

Yeah, that's fine with me.

Let me see.

Yeah, it's okay.

---

That sounds fine with me.

Yeah.

Yeah, right.

Uhuh.

---

Tell me about your date last night.

Well, it wasn't a date actually.

There's just nothing to tell.

Nothing particular. It was rather boring.

You won't believe it! It was just perfect!

---

What did you do ?

And, then, he didn't say a word.

That's all.

Guess what!

Then, he suddenly gave me this ring.

---

How embarrassing!

Yeah, but he is a good guy, I guess.

Yes, absolutely.

Yeah, but it was ok.

---

We kind of had some quality time together.

I'm envious of you!

Wow, that's good.

That's nice!

Are you gonna meet him again?

---

I hope you guys get along well.

That's what I hope.

I hope he will like me.

Well, who knows?

I hope so.

---

Unit 05

# Feeling

Talk in ENGLISH+

# Unit 05

# Feeling

## Pronounce it!

Coalescence 서로 융화되는 음들

/mm tt ss /

some milk some money that tall not talking half finished help Peter this shot give Vince should do this zoo this show ask Kim sit down

## Speak out!

I want some milk.

He wasn't that tall before.

We should do it now.

Let me ask Kim.

I'm not talking about it.

I really enjoyed this show.

They will leave now.

He was sleepy.

She sees Sally.

I need some money.

Does Bob believe that?

He returned to work.

## Tips!

▸ 두 단어(같은 자음끼리 혹은 다른 자음끼리)가 연이어 구강 내 어느 지점에서 발음될 때, 앞 단어가 발음 안 되는 경우가 생긴다. 두 발음이 서로 융합되어 일체가 되는 것이다.

## Situation 9 I need to be refreshed.

Mark: Hey, what's up?

Julie: I'm really depressed these days.
I don't know why.

Mark: Is that because you broke up with your boyfriend?

Julie: No, it's not that. I just think I'm missing something important in my life.

Mark: You see? I said you need a new boyfriend.

Julie: Hello, I said I am so over him!
I don't have any feelings for him at all.

Mark: Well, if you ask me, I can say this.
Look at those couples. They look so happy together. When they are together, I'm sure they feel they have everything.

Julie: I think she chose him because he's rich, if you ask me.
You see? He certainly isn't attractive to me!

Mark: Hmm··· Julie, what's got into you? You really need something to make you refreshed.

Julie: The point is I need something to improve my life. And I want to learn some different things.

Mark: And you know where I am, if you need me.

Julie: Thanks. I'm thinking of taking a trip to Canada for a while to meet my old friends. It will be great. I hope to spend time thinking of ways to better my life!

Mark: What can I say?
I guess you are just special. I cannot wait to see you with the better life you want.

Julie: Well, we should go back into the class again, and thank you.
I feel much better now.

Mark: Don't mention it. I want to say thank YOU for having a chance to talk to you.

## Say in English!

A: 무슨 일이야?
B: 기분이 우울해.

A: 뭔가 중요한 걸 놓치고 있는 것 같아.
B: 네가 필요하다면 내가 여기 있다는 거 알지?

A: 그녀는 그가 부자라서 그를 선택했을 거야
B: 갑자기 왜 그래?

A: 고마워. 기분이 훨씬 좋아졌어.
B: 천만에.

## Be brave!

depressed

How do you feel today?

I feel really depressed.

break up

What's wrong with you?

I broke up with my boyfriend.

attractive

Who is the most attractive girl in our class?

I think it's Jane.

miss

Who do you miss?

I miss my ex-boyfriend.

improve

What can I do to improve my English?

Practice it every day!

precious

What is the most precious thing in your life?

It's my little boy.

## Upgrade it!

**improve**

He's improved a lot!

I'm gonna improve my English.

**depressed**

I feel depressed.

Don't make yourself depressed.

**important**

This is a very important subject to study.

Do something important.

**break**

I don't wanna break the rule.

Let's take a break.

They just broke up.

**refresh**

I need something to refresh myself.

She felt refreshed.

There are some refreshments in the room.

**precious**

She is very precious to me.

She is crazy about precious stones.

I can say she is a very precious friend.

**special**

Do you want something special?

This is very special.

I don't want to read TV specials.

**mention**

Don't mention it.

Do you have anything to mention to me?

**chance**

Chances are, he's gonna survive.

I got a chance.

Fifty percent chance of shower today!

Thank you for giving me a chance.

| **Remember!** | **Write five expressions of your choice.** |
|---|---|
| 1. | |
| 2. | |
| 3. | |
| 4. | |
| 5. | |

## Situation 10 You look more human.

Julie: Are you okay? You look tired.

Jeff: I'm feeling under the weather.

Julie: Why don't you take a break?

Jeff: I can't. I have to finish this today.

Julie: You know you should take care of your health when you're still young.
Do you want some chocolate cookies and some tea?

Jeff: No. I lost my appetite.
Well, I'll just have a cup of tea then.

Julie: Okay, here you are. Be careful. It's very hot.

Jeff: Thanks. I feel much better now.

Julie: You know, you're impressing everyone. But you work too much.

Jeff: Do you think it's a problem?

Julie: No, but all work and no play makes you feel stressed.

Jeff: You're right.

Julie: By the way, what's that thing on your shirt?

Jeff: What? Gee··· it's coffee! I had coffee this morning.
This is my favorite shirt.

Julie: Don't worry. I'm sure we can get it off.

Jeff: I'm not myself today. You think I am terrible today, right?

Julie: No, it's not that. What can I say?
You look more human.

## Say in English!

A: 좀 쉬는 것 어때?
B: 이것을 다 끝마쳐야 해.

A: 초콜릿 좀 먹을래?
B: 아니, 그냥 차 한잔만 할래.

A: 넌 일을 너무 많이 해.
B: 그게 문제라고 생각해?

A: 셔츠에 묻은 것 그게 뭐야?
B: 이런! 커피잖아.

## Be brave!

look tired

What happened to you? You look very tired.

I had to stay up all night yesterday.

take care of

Who is taking care of your little boy?

His nanny.

take a break

Let's take a five-minute break. It's exhausting.

That's a good idea.

have coffee

How many cups of coffee did you have today?

I only had one.

too much

I drank ten cups of coffee today.

It's too much for one day!

feel stressed

When do you feel stressed?

When you ask me that kind of question.

## Upgrade it!

impress

You're impressing everyone.

He is very impressive.

She's always trying to impress others.

finish

I have to finish this today.

Just finish your meal.

Can you see the finish line there?

health

Keep your health while you're still young.

I go to the health club every evening.

He has some health problems.

This is the health care centre.

appetite

She has a big appetite.

I lost my appetite.

careful

Be careful!

She is a careful driver.

You need to be careful.

problem

No problem.

She has a big problem.

What's your problem?

favorite

This is my favorite subject.

What's your favorite food?

My favorite color is blue.

myself

Oh, no! I'm not myself today!

Look at yourself in the mirror.

I'll do it myself.

## Cultural Tip!

미국에서 약은 무조건 의사 처방전(prescription)이 있어야 살 수 있는 것으로 알고 있지만 그 외 처방전 없이 살 수 있는 over-the-counter drug도 있다. 우리가 약국에서 가볍게 구입하는 소화제(digestive), 1회용 반창고(bandage) 같은 것은 근처 대형 슈퍼마켓이나 편의점에서도 구입할 수 있다. 약국은 drugstore나 pharmacy라고 하며 drugstore에서는 약 외에 각종 잡화를 판다. Pharmacy는 약을 처방전대로 조제해 주는 곳이므로 의사 처방전을 들고 이곳으로 가면 된다. 어쨌든 미국은 병원비가 놀랄 만큼 비싸기 때문에 어지간한 중병이 아니면 병원에 잘 안 간다고 보면 된다. 우리처럼 병원에 쉽게 자주 가면 미국인들은 분명히 어디 중병에 걸렸다고 생각하고 놀랄 수 있다.

**Remember!** Write five expressions of your choice.

1.

2.

3.

4.

5.

## Survive Yourself!

What's up?

Nothing.

Something unexpected happened.

Hey, come over here.

Well, Jimmy and Jane broke up yesterday.

---

It's not that.

Then, what?

Ok, let's think it over later.

Ok, be honest!

---

I'm so over him!

Calm down.

What happened!

Do you really think so?

---

He doesn't look attractive to me.

Unbelievable.

Oh, but he is gorgeous to me!

Well, he is not your type, I guess.

---

What's got into you?

I don't want to talk about it now.

I lost my baggage.

---

I think I'm feeling under the weather.

You need some fresh air.

So do I.

Are you drowsy?

Cheer up!

---

You should take care of your health.

Thank you.

I know.

Yeah, I don't feel energetic these days.

---

What's that thing on your shirt?

Oh, it's coffee. I had coffee this morning.

Oh, my! I have stains here.

---

Unit 06

# Airport

Talk in ENGLISH+

# Unit 06

# Airport

## Pronounce it!

**/θ/ becomes /s/**

/θ - s z /

boss thinks meets Thursdays likes things his things gets thinner
adds things writers think guys think was thirsty

/θ - tʃ dʒ ʃ/

watch things match three such thoughts change things bridge things
charge through wash things push things fresh things

## Speak out!

The boss thinks he gets thinner day by day.

The class meets Thursdays.

He lived at this place thousands of years ago.

The guys think that it's not right.

The bird was thirsty.

Those are his things.

The writers think this book is terrible.

I want this thick one.

Whose things are those?

Just watch things for a while.

Let's match things up.

Such thoughts are not good for health.

Don't push things away.

Let's watch through the window.

The judge thought we were innocent.

## Tips!

- /θ/가 /s z/ 뒤에서 /s/로 변화된다. 이 때는 'th' 발음이 흔히 아는 /θ/ 발음이 안되고 평범하게 바뀐다.
- **/θ/**는 /tʃ dʒ ʃ/뒤에서 또한 /s/로 바뀐다.

## Situation 11 This airport is crowded.

Julie: This airport is always crowded!

Ann: Look out and keep all your bags close to you. They can easily be stolen.

Julie: Yeah, you can say that again.

Ann: You know, causing problems at the airport is just horrible to think about, especially when you are on a vacation.

Julie: I know, and where's the check in counter?
We should get our boarding passes.

Ann: It's right over there.
Isn't it better to wait for Mark?

Julie: He said he would be at the airport sometime soon. I just got his message.

Ann: Then, let's go to the counter first and be ready for ticketing.

Julie: We can wait for him there.

Ann: Is it the direct flight to Vancouver?

Julie: No. We're gonna stop in Tokyo and transfer to the connecting flight to Vancouver there.

Ann: Wow, I can hang around Tokyo while waiting then.

Julie: Well, we are not allowed to leave the airport. Or else, we must pay the tax again.

Ann: Hmm··· That's troublesome.
By the way, you just have two bags?

Julie: Yes, this suitcase, and I'll carry this small bag on with me.
Do you have three bags to check in?

Ann: No, these two. I'll carry this one with me.
I hope it is not overweight.

Julie: I don't think so.
Oh, here he comes at last! Hey, Mark, over here!

## Say in English!

A: 체크인 카운터가 어디 있지?
B: 바로 저기 있어.

A: Mark 를 기다리는 게 낫지 않겠어?
B: 그가 지금쯤 공항에 올 거라고 했어.

A: 직항이니?
B: 도쿄에서 연결편으로 갈아 탈 거야.

A: 가방이 딱 두 개뿐이야?
B: 응. 넌 체크인 할 가방이 세 개야?

## Be brave!

crowded

I don't like to be in a crowded place.

Me neither. I am agoraphobic. Are you too?

pay tax

Do I have to pay all these taxes? They are too much for me.

Don't grumble. It's your responsibility as a US citizen.

overweight

Can I carry this bag with me?

I'm afraid you can't. It's overweight.

get out of

How can I get out of this hell?

There is no way out. Just persevere.

at last

I found him at last.

What are you going to do with him?

board

Where do I board the ship?

Right over there.

## Upgrade it!

**crowded**

The city street is always crowded.

Look at the crowd!

**close**

They are close friends.

The airport is close to your house.

Come close to me.

**boarding**

They are boarding the plane.

Show me your boarding pass.

They are on board.

**still**

I'm still healthy.

Are you still at work?

**right**

He's right.

Turn right at the end of the street.

You spelled your name right.

**check**

Where's the check-in counter?

Please cash this check.

What do you want to check?

**transfer**

He transferred to another branch.

I will transfer to the connecting flight.

I will transfer to bus number 50.

**connect**

I'll connect you to this department.

This is the connecting flight.

Please connect me to the Personnel. Department

**Remember!** Write five expressions of your choice.

1.

2.

3.

4.

5.

## Situation 12 In-flight

**Ann:** Flight AA 701 to Vancouver Seat 24L.
Well, this is my first time to take an international flight.
It's thrilling!

**Mark:** It's almost the same as a domestic flight, but the in-flight meal is somewhat different on the menu.
Oh, I'm hungry.

**Ann:** I'm hungry, too. When do they serve lunch?

**Mark:** Mm··· I can smell chicken.
Oh, my stomach is rumbling now.

**Flight Attendant:** Hello.

**Mark:** Hi.

**Flight Attendant:** Chicken, salmon, or vegetarian?

**Mark:** Chicken, please.

**Flight Attendant:** Anything to drink?

**Mark:** Yes, some red wine, please.

**Flight Attendant:** Here you are.

**Mark:** Thank you.

**Flight Attendant:** And for you, ma'am? Chicken, salmon, or vegetarian?

**Ann:** Salmon, please.

**Flight Attendant:** And any drink?

**Ann:** Yes, just water, please.

**Flight Attendant:** With or without gas?

**Ann:** Sorry? I don't understand.

**Flight Attendant:** This is Evian without gas. And this is Perrier with gas.

**Ann:** Oh, yes. Evian, please.

**Flight Attendant:** Here you are. Enjoy your meal.

**Ann:** Thank you. Wow, it looks delicious!

**Mark:** Yes, I'm really enjoying it.

Oh, and don't forget to fill in your immigration card after your meal.

**Ann:** What's that?

**Mark:** They check your immigration card and your passport when you arrive, and ask a few questions.

**Ann:** Like what?

**Mark:** Like··· the purpose of your visit or the place you are staying, and so on.

**Ann:** All right. Uh, do you have a pen?

**Mark:** No, I don't, sorry. Julie may have one, I guess.

She's always well prepared.

## Say in English!

A: 국제선은 처음 타는 거야
B: 국내선과 거의 같아.

A: 언제 점심 주지?
B: 조만간 서비스할거야.

A: 마실 것 좀 드릴까요?
B: 네. 와인 좀 주세요.

A: gas 있는 걸로 드릴까요, 없는 것으로 드릴까요?
B: 없는 것으로 주세요.

## Be Brave!

thrilling

How thrilling was it when you were in Africa?

It's more than I can say.

somewhat

Tell me about your brothers.

They are somewhat different in their opinions.

rumble

What's the noise?

It's a heavy cart rumbling by.

delicious

What's the most delicious thing in the world?

There are too many to name.

vegetarian

Do you eat meat?

No, I am a vegetarian.

well-prepared

Are you well-prepared for the test?

Not really.

## Upgrade it!

flight

This is the connecting flight.

Flight AA 701 to Vancouver.

This is the last flight.

different

They are different.

This room is different from yours.

What's the difference?

It makes no difference.

international

They're going to attend the international conference.

This is the international airport.

I take the international flight.

anything

Just give me anything.

Anything to drink?

I don't like to do anything.

without

I cannot live without you.

I want some water without gas.

Without your help, I would not succeed.

enjoy

I really enjoyed the show.

Enjoy yourself.

prepared

I want to be prepared.

All things are prepared.

He is preparing something.

## Cultural Tip!

**미국 공항에 내려서 하는 대화**

영어권 나라에 처음 여행을 하게 되면 거치게 되는 곳이 바로 공항이다. 비행기에서 내려서 공항을 나가기까지 어떤 대화가 있을 수 있는지 알아보자.

입국 심사 때

| | |
|---|---|
| Next please. (다음 분) | 대기선에 있다 가면 된다. |
| Passport please. | 여권 좀 보여주세요. |
| Here you are. | 여기 있습니다. |
| Where are you from? | 어디서 오셨나요. |
| From Korea, Sir. | 한국서 왔습니다. (직원이 여자면 Ma'am 이라 함) |
| How long are you going to stay? | 얼마나 머물 것입니까? |
| I will stay 15 days. | 15일간 있을 예정입니다. |
| What is the purpose of your visit? | 방문목적은 무엇입니까? |
| Visit my friend. | 친구 방문입니다. |
| Where are you going to stay? | 어디서 묵을 예정입니까? |

이 때 친구의 주소를 불러 줘야 한다. 입국 시 방문지 주소기재가 의무사항이므로 반드시 동일하여야 한다.

**세관신고 할 때**

| | |
|---|---|
| Do you have anything to declare? | 신고 할 것 있습니까? |
| No, I don't. | 아니요, 없습니다. |
| Thank you. | 감사합니다. |

이 정도의 대화가 가능하면 영어권의 어느 나라에서도 공항의 이용에 어려움이 없을 것이다.

| **Remember!** | **Write five expressions of your choice.** |
|---|---|
| 1. | |
| 2. | |
| 3. | |
| 4. | |
| 5. | |

## Survive Yourself!

This airport is always crowded!

Yes, you're right.

Yeah, we should be careful.

Like this?

Oh, yeah?

---

Where's the check-in counter?

It's right over there.

Well, I'm a stranger here.

It's somewhere around here.

Sorry, I don't know.

---

Is it the direct flight to Vancouver?

Yes, that's right.

No, you should transfer to the connecting flight in Tokyo.

---

We are not allowed to leave the airport.

Why not?

Then, should we wait right at the airport?

Oh, I didn't know that.

---

This is my first time to take an international flight.

Me, too.

Well, I've taken it before.

Oh, are you sure?

---

My stomach is rumbling now.

You must be hungry.

Did you skip breakfast?

Do you want something to eat?

---

Don't forget to fill in your immigration card after your meal.

Oh, should I?

What is that?

But I don't know how.

---

She's always well prepared.

You can say that again.

That's what she is. Isn't she?

---

Unit 07

# Travel

Talk in **ENGLISH+**

# Unit 07

## Travel

### Pronounce it!

/ð/ becomes /z/

/ð/ - /s z /

kiss then  gets those  likes that  guess that  rides there  adds that  surprise the  raise the  why's that  is though

/ð/ - /tʃ dʒ ʃ/

watch those  bench that  catch that  judge those  change that
college they  wash these  wish their  push those

### Speak out!

Did you kiss then?
She likes that.
He rides there.
Why is that?
Can I use this?
Whose pen is this?
She needs these.
He wants the book.

Don't touch those.
Let's eat lunch there.
Can you cash this check?
I like a speech that's short.
There's a page that's missing.
Catch that dog!

### Tips!

- /ð/가 /s z/ 뒤에서 /z/로 변화된다. 이 때는 'th' 발음이 흔히 아는 /ð/ 발음이 안되고 평범하게 바뀐다.
- /ð /가 /tʃ dʒ ʃ/뒤에서 또한 /z/로 바뀐다.

## Situation 13 There are many attractions in this city.

Julie: I just want to look around before dinner.
Do you want to join me?

Ann: Sure, but what about Mike?

Julie: He stepped out to exchange some money.
I think he's just hanging around alone somewhere.
So, are you ready to go?

Ann: Yes. Where is the best place to look around?
I want to see a museum or park.

Julie: Let's drop by the Visitor's Center first.
We can get some information and some city maps there.

Ann: Okay, that's good.

Julie: I saw one right across the street. Oh, there it is.

Ann: You've been here in Vancouver, right?

Julie: Yes, but it was long ago.

Ann: Here we are.
Excuse me. Can I get a map of this city?

Clerk: Sure. Here it is.

Ann: Thanks. We have almost a month in this city. What places are good to look around?

Clerk: Well, there are beautiful parks along the beach and you can also enjoy the markets or concerts.
You can find all the places on the map.

Ann: Thanks. Where's the nearest market around here?

Clerk: You can see it on the map here.
There's one right past the theater.

## Say in English!

A: 나랑 같이 갈래?
B: 그래, 그런데 Mike는 어떻게 해?

A: 구경 다니기 좋은 곳이 어디지?
B: 여행자 센터에 가자.

A: 여기 예전에 와봤었지?
B: 응, 그렇지만 오래 전이야.

A: 이 도시 지도 좀 얻을 수 있을까요?
B: 물론이죠. 여기 있습니다.

## Be brave!

look around

Would you like to look around the city?

Sure. Could you show me around?

across

Where is the post office?

It's right across from the bank.

information

What kind of information do you need?

You don't have to bother. I can look for it myself.

long ago

When did you last see him?

It was so long ago!

the nearest

What's the nearest building to your apartment?

It's the financial building.

## Upgrade it!

**join**

Will you join us?

I'd like to join the tour.

**hang**

I just want to hang around.

Please hang it on the wall.

Don't hang up the phone.

The murderer was hanged last year.

**place**

This is my place.

Where is the best place to look around?

I like that place there.

**step**

He just stepped out.

Watch your step!

Just a few steps will take you to that place.

They went about the work step by step.

**information**

I need some information

Where is the Information Centre?

If you search the web, you can get a lot of information.

**several**

I have several questions to ask.

There are several beautiful parks.

Several people are standing out there.

**market**

The Stock Market has crashed.

I've got some stuff to buy at the market.

This is the marketplace.

**Remember!** Write five expressions of your choice.

1.

2.

3.

4.

5.

## Situation 14 I'd like to reserve tickets.

Mark: I was trying to get some information but the Internet was too slow.
I couldn't reserve tickets through the Internet.

Julie: That's okay. I'd rather buy tickets in person.
It is much more romantic. Do you have the Theater Guide book?

Mark: No, but I can see one here on this shelf.

Julie: Let me check the schedule.
How many shows do they have tonight?

Mark: Well, there are shows at 7:00 and 9:00.
I'm not sure if we can get tickets for tonight.
Why don't we reserve tickets for this Saturday?

Julie: You know I'm going on a camping trip to the Jasper area with my friends this Saturday.

Mark: Oh, is it this weekend?

Julie: Yes. If you want, you and Ann can also join us.

Mark: I'd love to.

Julie: Now, it's our turn. I think the 7:00 o'clock show will be better.

Mark: Okay. Hi, do you have tickets for the 7:00 o'clock show tonight?

Clerk: Yes. We still have a few seats left. How many, sir?

Mark: Just two, please. I'll pay by cash.

Clerk: All right. That's $36.

Mark: There you go. Oh, one more thing.
Are there any good tourist sites near here?
We still have 3 more hours.

Clerk: How about Starry Park?
You can take a walk and enjoy shopping for some souvenirs on the way.

Mark: Oh. That's a good idea. Thanks a lot.

Clerk: You're welcome.

## Say in English!

A: 오늘밤 몇 번의 공연이 있나요?
B: 7시와 9시에 공연이 있어요..

A: 이번 토요일로 표를 예약하는 게 어때?
B: 좋은 생각이야.

A: 이 근처에 좋은 관광지 있어요?
B: Starry Park 어때요?

A: 현금으로 지불 할게요.
B: 좋아요.

## Be brave!

**through**

How did you reserve your seats?

Through the Internet.

**turn**

Who's next?

It's my turn.

**left**

How many seats are left?

I'm afraid not many.

**romantic**

Do you think romantic love exists?

Well, I have never thought about it. Give me some time to think it over.

**souvenir**

I bought some souvenirs on my trip to Korea.

That's awesome. What is mine?

**pay by cash**

Do I have to pay by cash?

No, we also take credit cards.

## Upgrade it!

**reserve**

The table is reserved.

I'd like to reserve a seat.

Have you reserved a table for dinner?

**through**

I can't get through.

This tunnel goes through the city.

You should look through the file.

**ticket**

I got a speeding ticket.

Do you have tickets for the show?

Tickets, please.

**show**

He just showed up.

I want to enjoy tonight's show.

What time is the first show?

Just show it to me.

**cash**

Will you cash this for me?

Cash or credit card?

I'll pay by cash.

**way**

This way, please.

Is this the right way to go?

This is the way he made a lot of money.

**souvenir**

This is the souvenir shop.

I want some souvenirs for my son.

It can be a souvenir.

## Cultural Tip!

여행을 하면 낯선 사람과 많은 만남을 가지게 된다. 그럴수록 서로에 대한 예절을 지키는 것이 중요하다.

많은 사람이 있는 곳에서 줄을 서는 것은 아주 당연한 일이다. 우리나라에서도 이제 많이 보편화되기는 하지만 주위 사람을 먼저 생각하는 것은 어느 나라든지 나쁠 것이 없다. Please stand in line!

관광 중에 사진 촬영 금지나, 출입 금지 등의 사항에 대해서는 반드시 지켜야 한다. 그렇지 않을 경우 그 곳을 떠날 것을 요청 받을 준비를 해야 한다. 이런 말을 듣지 않기를 바란다. I ask you to leave here. 미국 사회는 lady first를 대부분 실천한다. 엘리베이터를 타거나 내릴 때, 에스컬레이터에서, 차를 탈 때, 방 출입 시 여성을 먼저 배려한다. After you!

**Remember!** Write five expressions of your choice.

1.

2.

3.

4.

5.

## Survive Yourself!

Do you want to join me?

If it's okay with you.

Well, if you don't mind.

Sure.

Ok, let's go.

---

Where is the best place to look around?

There are so many beautiful places around here.

Central Park is very nice.

Well, you can ask Lisa.

---

Let's go to the Visitor's Center first!

That's a good idea.

Okay.

By the way, where is the Visitor's Center?

---

You've been here before, right?

Yeah, just once.

Yes, I've been here several times.

No, this is my first visit here.

---

Can I get a map of this city?

Sure.

It's over there on the counter.

Okay, just take one copy.

---

It was long ago.

How long?

Oh, yeah?

Ok, go ahead.

---

Where's the nearest market around here?

I'm new here myself.

You can walk that way.

It's just one stop by bus.

Sorry, I don't know.

---

You can see it on your map.

Oh, really?

Wow, that's great.

Let me see it.

Where?

---

Unit 08

# Direction

# Unit 08

# Direction

## Pronounce it!

**/t/ dropped after /n/**

/n/ - /t/

plenty winter hunter county center counter identify painter

point at hunt her want to sent her count her paint her

## Speak out!

There's plenty of food.

Winter vacation is coming around.

He lives in Malcolm County.

It's in the center.

Put it on the counter.

He's pointing at her.

I want to paint her.

Let's paint it blue.

She wanted to go.

I've only got twenty dollars.

Who would identify the difference?

## Tips!

▸ /t/앞에 /n/이 있으면 /t/가 발음되지 않고, /n/음은 flapping(/N/) 되어 버린다. 이 때 /n/음은 매우 빨리 발음된다.

## Situation 15 Turn right at the end of the street.

Mark: Will you take a walk to Starry Park?
Julie: Starry Park? Okay. That's good.
Mark: We can enjoy bike riding and the beautiful beach there.
Julie: That's a good idea.
Mark: We can have dinner at the nearby restaurant after that.
Julie: Yeah. Do you know which way we should go to the park?
Mark: Let me ask.
Excuse me. How can I get to Starry Park from here?
Man: Well, it's not far. You can walk that way.
Just go straight.
Mark: Thank you so much.
Man: No trouble.
Mark: Now, we should go this way from here as he said.
Look! I can see the sign.
Julie: Right. But it says 200 meters. I think that's too far.
Mark: It's okay. We can enjoy the city street while walking.
Julie: You're right. The map says we should turn right at the end of this street.
And it goes to the park.
Mark: Oh, look! There are street musicians.
Julie: Wow, it's amazing.
Mark: They don't look like amateurs.
Julie: Right. Their music is just great.
Mark: Julie, I can see the bike rental shop here.
Julie: Why don't we walk a little more? Now I remember this area.
If we turn right, there's another store. The rental price here is much cheaper.
Mark: Okay. You mean that place over there?
Julie: There it is.
It's perfect weather to ride a bike.
Mark: Yeah, I'm really expecting it. Let's go.

## Say in English!

A: Starry Park까지 걸을까요?

B: 좋은 생각이야.

A: 여기서 Starry Park까지 어떻게 가나요?

B: 그다지 멀지 않습니다.

A: 저기 보이는 저곳 말이니?

B: 그래. 저기야.

A: 자전거 타기에 완벽한 날씨야..

B: 그래. 정말 기대 돼.

## Be brave!

ride a bike

Can you ride a bike?

No, I have never learned how.

get to

How do I get to the airport?

You can take a cab. It takes only 30 minutes.

remember

Don't you remember the words we exchanged?

I am sorry, but I don't remember any.

nearby

Where do we eat dinner after the show?

At a nearby restaurant.

another

Could I have another cup of coffee?

Sure, here you go.

much cheaper

This is much cheaper than that, don't you think?

Yeah, I totally agree with you.

## Upgrade it!

ride

Let's ride a bike.

Give me a ride.

take

I need to take a break.

Will you take a walk?

I'll take you to the market.

nearby

The airport is nearby.

I can't find anything nearby.

straight

She has straight hair.

Go straight.

Keep it straight.

while

Don't move while sitting.

Will you feed my puppy while you are here?

I'll be away for a while.

amazing

It's an amazing show.

What an amazing sky!

She is amazing.

perfect

I want to make it perfect.

He is a perfect man.

It's perfect!

expect

He's expecting you.

I expect to see you.

You make me expect something unusual in life.

| **Remember!** | Write five expressions of your choice. |
|---|---|
| 1. | |
| 2. | |
| 3. | |
| 4. | |
| 5. | |

## Situation 16 Can you show me where I am?

Ann: Well, she said 100 meters from the post office, but… Gee, it's not right.
Excuse me. Can I ask you something?

Man: Sure.

Ann: I'm lost. Can you help me?

Man: Sure, you're on the corner of Main Street and Park Avenue.

Ann: Can you show me where I am on this map?

Man: Okay. Let's see… Now you are here at this point on the map.

Ann: I'm looking for the Central Theater.
Can you show me the way to the theater?

Man: Um… This way goes to Starry Park and I know it's just near here.

Ann: Yeah, I've heard it's somewhere around here.

Man: Well, I don't know exactly. I'm not from here myself, either.
There's a police officer standing there. Why don't you ask him?

Ann: OK. Thanks anyway.

Man: Bye.

Ann: Excuse me, officer.

Officer: Yes, ma'am.

Ann: I need some help. I'm going to the Central Theater.
Is it this direction?

Officer: Oh, it's right over there.
You see the big signboard there?

Ann: Yes?

Officer: That's the theater you're looking for.

Ann: Oh, it's very near! Thank you so much.

Officer: My pleasure.

## Say in English!

A: 뭘 좀 여쭤봐도 되요?
B: 물론요.

A: 길을 잃었어요.
B: Main Street와 Park Avenue의 모퉁이에 있습니다.

A: 지도상에서 어디인지 알려주시겠어요?
B: 여기 이 지점에 있어요.

A: 이 근처 어디라고 들었는데.
B: 저도 여기 출신이 아니어서요.

## Be brave!

show

Could you show me the way?

Sure, just go straight ahead.

look for

What are you looking for?

I am looking for my pen.

around here

Where is the theater?

It's somewhere around here on this map.

exactly

Tell me exactly what happened.

I only have a vague idea.

signboard

Can you read the signboard?

No, it's too far away!

lost

I got lost. I don't know where I am now.

Ask the police officer standing there.

## Upgrade it!

**lost**

Where's the Lost and Found?

I'm lost!

She lost her baggage.

**somewhere**

It's somewhere around here.

Are you going somewhere this summer?

**exactly**

Tell me exactly what it is.

It's exactly the same.

I cannot answer exactly.

**anyway**

Thanks anyway.

Anyway, I'm not going.

**direction**

I'm going this direction.

Is this the direction you want?

Let's ask for the directions.

**pleasure**

My pleasure.

It's a pleasure to help you.

**map**

Look at the map.

Do you have the route map?

Let's buy a city map.

I don't know where I am on this map.

## Cultural Tip!

미국의 혼잡한 거리에서 street musician을 보는 것은 결코 어려운 일이 아니다. 우리나라에서도 가끔씩 외국 사람들이 대학가에서 음악을 연주하거나 묘기를 부리면서 지나가는 사람들의 시선을 잡기도 한다.

이러한 street musician도 여러 종류가 있다. 첫 번째는 순수 아마추어인 가난한 음악가들이다. 이들은 지나가는 사람들이 어떻게 생각하든 또 그들이 그 음악에 감동되어 약간의 관람료를 던져 주고 가든 말든 자신의 음악에 심취되어 연주한다. 자신들의 음악을 홍보하고 여러 사람들이 즐기는 것을 목적으로 한다.

두 번째는 순수하게 돈을 버는 것이 목적인 프로 음악가들이다. 이들은 나름대로의 노하우를 갖고 고객을 끌기 위한 노하우를 가지고 있다. 예를 들면 사람들이 많이 다니는 몇 군데 정해 놓고 요일 별로 돌아가며 공연을 한다. 매일 같은 장소에서 연주를 하는 것보다는 이곳 저곳을 다니면 돈을 번다.

세 번째는 여행을 하면서 현지에서 여행경비를 조달할 목적으로 장사를 벌이는 아르바이트 음악사들이다. 이들의 연주 실력은 위의 두 부류보다 떨어져서 수입은 떨어지지만 대신 이들은 악기나 노래뿐만 아니라 이상한 옷차림이나 꼼짝하지 않고 버티는 마네킹 흉내내기 (statue mime) 등을 선보여 사람들의 시선을 끈다.

**Remember!** Write five expressions of your choice.

1.

2.

3.

4.

5.

## Survive Yourself!

Will you take a walk to Starry Park?

No, it's too far.

Oh, come on. My leg hurts.

Ok. We can look around on the way.

---

Which way should we go to the park?

This way, I guess.

Let's ask him.

You mean we got lost?

---

It's not far.

Oh, good.

I'm completely exhausted.

But the map says it's one hour walking distance.

---

Can I ask you something?

Sure.

Yes?

Why not.

Yeah, go ahead.

Yes, what is it?

---

I don't know where I am.

Hmm we're somewhere around here on the map.

You see? We're right over here.

Neither do I.

Let's ask someone.

---

I'm not from here myself.

I'm not, either.

Oh, but your accent is British.

---

You are here at this point.

Oh, at last.

You mean this spot here?

Thanks.

---

Why don't you ask him?

That's a good idea.

But he looks like a stranger here.

---

Unit 09

# Health & Diet

Talk in **ENGLISH+**

# Unit 09

# Health & Diet

## Pronounce it!

/d/ dropped after /n/

/n/ - /d/

sounding understand candy wonder spending rounded

hand it kind of find out understand it around it

## Speak out!

Good spending habits are important.

It rounded well.

Please hand it to me.

I don't understand it.

We are kind of busy at the moment.

Let's find out about it.

We had a wonderful time.

Would you like some candy?

Let's find out the right answer.

## Tips!

▸ /d/앞에 /n/이 있으면 /d/가 발음되지 않고, /n/음은 flapping(/N/) 되어 버린다. 물론 이 때 강세는 /n/음이 있는 음절에 있어야 하며 매우 빨리 발음된다.

## Situation 17 I am on a diet.

Brian: Hi Julie, Long time no see. How have you been?

Julie : Hi, Brian! I have been busy because of my new project.

Brian: By the way, you look different but I am not quite sure what it is.

Julie : Well, I lost five kilos. I always wanted to lose these extra kilos.

Brian: Wow, great! How did you do it? Were you on any special diet program? Let me guess, the Atkins Diet?

Julie : No, it is outdated now. I have been on a juice fasting program.

Brian: I heard a lot of Hollywood stars love the program.

Julie : Yeah, it is good for people who want to lose weight in a relatively short period of time.

Brian: I am on a diet too.

Julie : Really? But you look the same. How long? What kind? Did you lose some weight?

Brian: I just started it yesterday. I would call it a "one meal a day" diet.

Julie : Wow, you mean you only eat one meal a day?
How long are you going to do that?

Brian: For about a month maybe. I only eat lunch. I really hate this extra fat, especially around my belly.

Julie : Well, I don't think it is good for your metabolism.
Some people even say that you should eat every three hours and five times a day to burn the calories more efficiently.

Brian: Really?
I think I have to visit an expert and ask for professional tips.

Julie : Please do that. I can recommend someone for you.
He is very popular and you have to arrange for a meeting at least two months ahead. I think he is fully booked now.
Besides, soon it is bikini season and everyone is getting ready for it.

Brian: Oh, he must make good money.

Julie : You can say that again! Here's his business card.
Call him right away!

Brian: I will do that. Thanks. See you later.

Julie : Bye, good luck!

## Say in English!

A: 어떻게 지내셨어요?
B: 바빴어요.

A: 뭔가 달라 보이는데요.
B: 5킬로 감량을 했어요.

A: 살을 좀 빼셨나요?
B: 어제 시작한 걸요.

A: 얼마나 하실 건가요?
B: 약 한달 정도요.

A: 당장 그에게 전화해 보세요.
B: 그러겠습니다.

## Be brave!

extra

Why do you need extra money?
I have to buy a present for my girlfriend.

on a diet

You look pale. What's wrong with you?
I am on a diet.

look the same

You guys look the same.
At a glance we look alike, but there are actually some differences.

hate

Why do you hate me?
Because you stole my boyfriend.

metabolism

She has such a slow metabolism.
That's why it's hard for her to lose weight.

fast

Do you ever fast?
No, never!

## Upgrade it!

**hate**

I hate you because I love you so much!

Who do you hate?

I don't hate anybody.

**expert**

He is an expert on that matter.

You should become an expert in at least one field.

How long does it take to become a true expert?

**meal**

How many meals do you eat a day?

I make it a rule to have three square meals a day.

He has not eaten even one meal today.

**recommend**

What do you recommend for my mother's birthday?

I recommend him as your assistant.

**extra**

Why do you need some extra money?

I will pay extra if you do as I say.

You should be extra careful with this one.

**only**

I only eat vegetables, not meat.

You are the only one for me.

The only way to get blessed is this.

**outdated**

That style is outdated.

For some students, e-mail is already outdated.

It's an outdated expression.

**popular**

He is popular among girls.

Who is the most popular in this class?

The novel is not popular any longer.

times

How many times do you pray a day?

How many times do you eat a day?

I eat three times a day.

ahead

He is far ahead of me.

My parents are ahead of the times.

Who is ahead of you in line?

weight

I need to lose weight.

How much weight did you lose last month?

He needs to gain some weight.

| **Remember!** | **Write five expressions of your choice.** |
|---|---|
| 1. | |
| 2. | |
| 3. | |
| 4. | |
| 5. | |

## Situation 18 My father's so demanding!

Julie : Hi Brian! Did you call the guy I recommended to you the other day?

Brian: No, I couldn't. I've been really busy because of my father.

Julie : What's up with your father?

Brian: He sprained his ankle while he was tending the garden.

Julie : Oh, no! Is he okay now?

Brian: He is getting better and better every day.
But I have to be by his side all the time doing errands for him.
I am even tending the garden myself in the sun while he is telling me what to do! And he is so demanding and never satisfied with my work.

Julie : That must be a lot of work.

Brian: You wouldn't believe it if you saw it with your own eyes.
I have no personal life now. I mean, not at all.
I have to move my body all day long. What a life!

Julie : There is no use complaining about it. Try to look at the positive side.

Brian: What do you mean? What is positive about it?

Julie : You are helping your father and exercising at the same time.
Some people spend huge money just to get some exercise.

Brian: That's different! They are exercising and relaxing but I'm working. And it gives me stress.

Julie : You don't have to separate work from exercise. I heard on the radio that Australians' most preferred job is being a carpenter. They think carpentry makes you exercise and earn money at the same time.

Brian: Killing two birds with one stone? That makes sense!
But still, it makes me crazy living for my father around the clock.
I know I am supposed to be more than willing to help my sick father. But

I need my freedom.

Julie : I understand. Have some patience. It won't last forever.

Brian: Yeah, you are right. I am not a good son to complain about such a thing. I think I should repent.

Julie : Come on. Don't blame yourself. Everyone would feel the same in your shoes. God will understand.

Brian: Well, I am not so sure, though.

## Say in English!

A: 그 사람한테 전화해봤어?
B: 아니 못했어.

A: 아버지께 무슨 일이라도 생겼니?
B: 발목을 삐셨어.

A: 아버지 지금은 괜찮으시니?
B: 매일 좋아지고 계셔.

A: 자책하지마.
B: 음... 하지만 잘 모르겠어.

## Be brave!

recommend

What do you recommend for dinner?

What about grilled shrimp?

do errands

Why didn't you appear at the meeting?

I had to do some errands for my father.

sprain

Why are the bandages all around your wrist?

I sprained it while playing tennis.

repent

Do you repent your sins?

Not if I can't understand what they are.

positive

Are you sure he will come?

Yes, I'm positive.

## Upgrade it!

sprain

I sprained my wrist while playing basketball.

He sprained his ankle while playing soccer.

A sprained ankle is a very common injury.

tend

They are tending to sick children in India.

My father tends the garden as a hobby.

Korean boys tend to be more aggressive than Japanese ones.

better

Your English is getting better every day.

I am getting better at English.

You had better get used to it.

personal

I need a personal life.

That is personal information. I won't give it to you.

Don't take it personally.

complain

You always complain about something.

Complaining does not help at all.

Why don't you stop complaining now?

positive

Be positive!

Get a positive view of life!

Positive people tend to be more successful.

same

They look the same.

The results are the same as before.

The same thing happened to me last night.

spend

How much money do you spend a month?

How would you like to spend the remaining time?

You have to be very careful with the money you spend.

I spent the whole weekend doing homework.

**separate**

They are separated now.

Separation is painful.

A fence separates the two gardens.

**mean**

Do you really mean it?

I mean it.

What do you mean by that?

**carpenter**

Jesus Christ was a carpenter.

To be a carpenter, you need special skills.

Is there anyone who wants to be a carpenter here?

## Cultural Tip!

미국은 DIY (Do It Yourself)의 천국이다. 홈 디포 (Home Depot)라는 곳은 없는 재료가 없을 정도로 아주 크고 이곳에서 많은 미국인들이 DIY를 위한 재료를 준비한다. 전문가에게 의뢰하면 아주 많은 돈을 지불해야 하는 것에 대한 경제적인 부담과 직접 자신의 손으로 자신의 집을 돌보는 두 마리의 새를 동시에 잡을 수 있기 때문이다. 예를 들어 견적이 5,000달러도 넘는 집 안뜰 공사를 직접 할 경우, 재료비는 10분의1도 채 들지 않는다. 혼자 할 수 없는 일은 친구들을 불러서 같이 하고 수고한 친구들을 위한 바비큐 파티 비용까지 합하더라도 총 비용이 1,000달러가 채 들지 않을 것이다. 미국은 노동에 대한 임금이 상당히 높기 때문인 것도 그 돈이 이렇게나 절약되는 이유이다.

**Remember!** Write five expressions of your choice.

1.

2.

3.

4.

5.

## Survive Yourself!

I think I have to visit an expert.

What for?

You're right.

You'd better visit him right now.

---

I can recommend someone for you.

Well, do you have someone in mind?

Ok, thank you.

I need someone reliable.

---

Call him right away!

But I'm sure he's not in at the moment.

No, we'd better wait and see.

Ok, do you know his number?

Hmm.. I think his number is somewhere in this pocket. Oh, here it is!

Long time, no see.

Yeah, it's been a long time.

Yeah, how have you been?

Yeah, what have you been up to?

Yeah, anything new?

He is getting better and better every day.

That's good news.

Hmm.. good to hear that.

What else?

I have to be by his side.

Why is that?

Is that so?

Well, if you want.

You are so kind.

I have no personal life now.

You are not complaining now, right?

But you are satisfied with your work.

Sorry to hear that.

That makes sense.

You see?

That's what I'm saying.

# Unit 10
# Events

Talk in ENGLISH+

# Unit 10

## Events

### Pronounce it!

**Dissimilation**

/r, n/ - /Ø/

government surprise northerner library secretary governor enterprise

thermometer corner February larger

### Speak out!

The new government will be set up.

I'm preparing a surprise party for him.

Will you stay at the library?

We need a new secretary in our office.

Do you have a thermometer in your place?

I need a larger room.

He was born in February.

Winter is just around the corner.

### Tips!

▸ 이화현상은 구어체의 격식 없는 영어에서 한 단어에서 /r/ 이나 /n/ 의 반복을 피하기 위해 불규칙적으로 일어난다.

## Situation 19 My parents' wedding anniversary is coming

Laura : Are you free this afternoon?

Julie : Well, I have no special plans yet. Why do you ask?

Laura : I really want you to do me a favor.

Julie : What do you want from me?

Laura : Come with me to the department store.

Julie : You mean, you want some help with shopping?

Laura : Yeah, exactly! My parents' wedding anniversary is coming up. Actually it's next Monday!

It will be easier if you help me select the presents.

Julie : Great! So what are you thinking of buying for them?

Laura : A scarf for my mom and a tie for my dad. What do you think?

Julie : Good! I bought the same things for my parents' wedding anniversary last month. Let's get moving. I have only three hours.

I don't want to miss the 7:30 show. It's my favorite.

Laura : Sure, it won't take long.

We can enjoy the show together at my house after shopping.

Let's order some Chinese food and enjoy it with the show.

Julie : That's perfect!

You know I love Chinese food.

I haven't had it for almost a month because my mom hates it.

Laura : My parents are not coming home until after the show.

We have plenty of time to enjoy ourselves.

Julie : I'm so glad to have a friend like you.

My mother never allows me to eat while watching TV.

## Say in English!

A: 오늘 오후에 시간되니?

B: 아직 별 약속은 없는데 왜 그래?

A: 내가 어떻게 해 주길 바라니?

B: 나랑 같이 백화점에 가자.

A: 부모님께 뭘 사줄까 생각하고 있니?

B: 엄마는 스카프 아빠는 넥타이.

A: 너와 같은 친구를 둬서 너무 기뻐.

B: 도움이 필요하면 언제든지 전화해.

## Be brave!

do a favor

Would you do me a favor?

Of course. Tell me.

take long

How long does it take to finish the project?

We are not sure yet.

anniversary

When is your 10th wedding anniversary?

It's this coming Friday.

order

What do you order?

I will wait until he comes.

plenty of

Are we in a hurry?

No, we still have plenty of time.

## Upgrade it!

free

I am free from 10 to 11 this morning.

Are you free tomorrow?

If you were free now, what would you do?

favor

Will you do me a favor?

Do me a favor, please!

Can I ask you a favor?

miss

I will miss the class because I have to go to the hospital.

Will you miss me after I am gone?

The cat is missing.

favorite

What is your favorite drink?

My favorite movie star is Jang Dong-gun.

Math is my favorite.

allow

You are not allowed to sit here.

My mother does not allow me to go shopping alone.

Would you allow me to go home now?

special

Do you have any special plans for tomorrow?

You are so special!

Is he someone special to you?

order

Let's order some food. I am hungry.

What would you order for me?

Anybody who ordered pepperoni pizza here?

plenty

We have plenty of time before the class starts.

He has plenty of money.

Money is never too plenty.

take

It will take about two hours.

It took only half an hour to complete the assignment.

Take it or leave it.

enjoy

Did you enjoy the party last night?

Let's enjoy ourselves at the picnic.

perfect

He is so perfect for me.

You can't be perfect in everything.

There is no perfect solution for the problem.

| **Remember!** | **Write five expressions of your choice.** |
|---|---|
| 1. | |
| 2. | |
| 3. | |
| 4. | |
| 5. | |

## Situation 20 I'm getting engaged!

Laura : Hello, this is Laura speaking. Can I speak to Julie please?

Julie : Hi, Laura! This is me, Julie.

Laura : I thought it was your mother.

I always have a problem recognizing your voice.

You and your mother sound the same.

Julie : Is that so? Everyone who calls my house says the same. What's up?

Laura : Oh, something big is up. You won't believe it. I am getting engaged!

Julie : What? Oh my God! You mean you are getting engaged to Mark?

Or is there another guy?

Laura : Come on! Mark is the only guy for me.

You know how crazy I am about Mark.

I am the fiance of Mark, *MY* Mark! I am so excited!

Julie : You should be. Tell me about the details.

Did he ask you to marry him? Or was it the other way around?

Laura : Of course it was him asking me to marry him.

You know how long I have waited for this to happen.

After six years, he finally proposed to me.

Julie : When did it happen? And where?

Laura : An hour ago in the park near my house. We were sitting on the bench and he suddenly took out roses from his bag and kneeled down in front of me, asking, "Will you marry me?"

Isn't it so romantic?

Julie : Wow, it is not like him.

I always thought that he is kind of unromantic and cool-headed.

Laura : I thought the same. I still can't believe it. You will never imagine how many times I pinched my arm to see if it was real.

We are going to have a small engagement party this weekend.

And we are going to get married as soon as he finishes his military service.

Julie : I am so envious of you guys. Am I invited? And who else are you going to invite?

Laura : We are inviting about ten people including you.

It is really a small party just among very close friends.

## Say in English!

A: 무슨 일이라도 있니?
B: 그럼 무슨 일이 있지.

A: 언제 일어난 일이야?
B: 한 시간 전이야.

A: 너무 낭만적이지 않니?
B: 야 그답지 않다.

A: 다른 남자라도 있니?
B: Mark가 내겐 유일한 남자야.

## Be brave!

**recognize**

Do you recognize me? We met at the school party the other night.

Sorry, I was drunk then. What was your name again?

**take out**

What are you doing? Get your hands off your purse.

I am just trying to take my ID out.

**pinch**

Ouch! Who pinched my arm?

Nobody. It's only the little bug crawling there.

**finally**

I finally got permission from mom.

Congratulations!

**engagement**

When is your engagement party?

We are not having one.

## Upgrade it!

**sound**

You sound sick.

Do I sound okay?

Does it sound okay to you?

**engage**

I got engaged to your father when I was only 20.

This is my engagement ring.

I am engaged to Mark.

**invite**

How many people are you inviting to the party?

Is he invited to your birthday party?

He invited me to his house.

**kneel**

I forgave him because he kneeled and asked for mercy.

Do not kneel on the floor. It's very dirty.

Let's kneel and pray to God.

**include**

It's all five of us including you.

The meal includes coffee and dessert.

The cost does not include the airfare.

**married**

Are you married or not?

How old were you when you got married?

I am married to an American citizen.

**happen**

The accident happened two hours ago.

It can happen to anybody.

I happened to see your boyfriend on the way home.

**suddenly**

Suddenly it came to my mind.

He suddenly appeared out of nowhere.

Suddenly, he burst into laughter.

envious

I am envious of you.

Everyone is envious of his talents.

I am not envious of anybody. I am content as I am now.

pinch

I pinched my thigh to stay awake.

The shoes pinch me at the heels.

Pinch me on my hand.

imagine

You can never imagine what happened.

You are free to imagine there is no hell but it exists.

Just imagine how happy I was!

## Cultural Tip!

**영국의 차문화**

영국 사람들은 아침식사 후, 오전 11시 경, 점심식사 후, 오후 4~5시경의 Afternoon Tea, 그리고 저녁식사 후 등, 이렇게 하루에 5번은 홍차를 마실 정도로 차를 좋아한다. 영국에서 차 문화가 번성하게 된 이유 중 하나는 영국의 식민지였던 인도의 영향이 크고, 이 때문에 영국에서는 주로 인도산 차와 실론차를 즐겨 마신다.

영국인들은 17세기 초에 런던에 커피하우스가 생기면서 차보다 커피를 먼저 접했지만, 커피를 재배할 수 있는 해외 식민지가 없었기 때문에 수급이 원활하지 못하자 중국으로 눈을 돌려 차를 들여온 1730년경부터 본격적인 차의 대중화가 이뤄졌다. 오후에 우아한 차 한 잔을 나누며 담소를 나누는 풍습은 영국의 귀족인 베드포드 공작부인 Anna에게서 시작됐다. 18세기 영국 상류 사회의 만찬은 주로 늦은 저녁 시간대에 열렸는데 이 시간까지 기다릴 수 없었던 공작부인은 오후에 친구들을 초대해 한 잔의 차를 마시며 여러 이야기를 주고 받았다. 이런 차 문화는 재빨리 영국 상류 사회에 유행처럼 번지기 시작했고 19세기에 들어서는 중류층까지 이를 받아들이면서 하나의 전통으로 자리 잡아가게 되었다.

| **Remember!** | Write five expressions of your choice. |
|---|---|
| 1. | |
| 2. | |
| 3. | |
| 4. | |
| 5. | |

## Survive Yourself!

Are you free this afternoon?

- I'm a little busy this afternoon.
- Why do you ask?
- Yes, I'm free after 2:00pm.
- Well, I don't have any particular appointment.

---

I have no special plans yet.

- Oh, good.
- Then, will you give me a hand?
- Well, then, will you join us for dinner?

---

I really want you to do me a favor.

- I would if I could.
- What is it?
- Sure, go ahead.
- Sorry, but I'm busy at the moment.

What do you want from me?

Nothing.

Well, if it's no trouble with you, I want you to join us for the meeting tomorrow.

He proposed to me.

How nice!

What good news!

Are you sure?

No way!

It's not like him.

Yeah, you're right.

But he is that kind of person.

That's because he loves you.

You won't believe it.

What about!

What do you mean?

What are you gonna talk about?

I thought the same.

Good.

Thank you for saying so.

Did you ask him to marry you?

No, I didn't.

No, it's not me.

Yes, I realized that I love her.

Unit 11

# Trouble

# Unit 11

## Trouble

**Pronounce it!** **/t/ /d/ changes into /D/**

/t / - /D/

butter water forty city letter meeting met them but he

/d/ - /D/

pudding radio ladder Friday leader wedding could have instead of

**Speak out!**

/t / - /D/

I want some bread and butter.

I want some water.

It is the letter from the lost city!

I've got to go.

She's really beautiful.

They let him go.

We ought to go to school.

He's buying a lot of books.

My English is getting better.

### /d/ - /D/

Did you eat the pudding on the table?

I heard his voice on the radio.

She did it instead of me.

Mary could have bought it.

He should have studied harder.

I could have done that.

## Tips!

- /t/음이 모음이나 /r/ 뒤에 있고, 뒤에 강세가 없는 모음 앞에 오면 flapping /D/ 음으로 변한다.
- /d/음이 모음이나 /r/ 뒤에 강세가 없는 음절 앞에 오면 flapping /D/ 음으로 변한다.

## Situation 21 I had a fight with my boyfriend!

Laura : Julie, you look terrible! Is anything wrong?

Julie : Yeah, I had a fight with my boyfriend.

Laura : That's too bad. Was it serious? Who started it?

Julie : Well, listen. This is what happened. I was preparing for my test in the library and Tommy came over and asked me to go out for dinner.

But it was only five o'clock and I did not want to get interrupted for another hour.

Laura: So, you said no, right?

Julie : Yes, and I asked him to come back an hour later.

And he suddenly got angry and yelled at me.

Laura: You mean in the library?

Julie : Yeah, there were a lot of people and I was so embarrassed.

I don't want to see him again.

Laura : How did you respond?

Julie : I just packed my things and hurried out. He tried to follow me but I didn't even look at his face and ran away.

Laura : Did he call?

Julie : Yeah, several times. But I didn't want to talk to him.

Laura : So, what are you going to do now?

Julie : I am going to break up with him.

I can never understand a man yelling in public places, no matter what!

What do you think?

Laura : I totally agree with you.

But he has been so well-mannered and I don't understand why he did that. Is he going through some personal crises?

Julie : I don't want to even think about it. You know how it feels to get scowled at by all the students in the library. It was so horrible.

**Laura :** Calm down and go see a movie or something for a change.

**Julie :** I want to, but I can't. I have to study.

**Laura :** That's too bad. Is there anything I can do for you?

Will you feel better if I buy you a nice dinner?

**Julie :** You are so sweet, but I don't think I can eat any food right now.

I am so upset.

## Say in English!

A: 너는 어떻게 생각해?
B: 네 말에 전적으로 동감이야.

A: 어떻게 할 거니?
B: 그와 헤어질 거야.

A: 무슨 일이라도 있니?
B: 남자 친구랑 싸웠어.

A: 진정하고 기분전환을 위해 영화를 보든지 해.
B: 그러고 싶지만, 안돼. 공부해야 하거든.

## Be brave!

have a fight

Why the long face?

I had a fight with my closest friend.

get angry

Why did he get angry?

Nobody knows.

respond

Will you respond to my question?

Just wait a second. I need some time to think.

well-mannered

I have never seen such a well-mannered man in my entire life.

You see he is from Europe.

yell

Did you yell at me?

No, I wasn't yelling. I was just expressing my opinion loudly.

## Upgrade it!

**sweet**

That's so sweet of you.

The coffee's so sweet. How many spoonfuls of sugar did you put in it?

If you eat too many sweets, you will have cavities.

**upset**

I am so upset because you rejected my offer.

I have an upset stomach.

If you feel upset, try to cheer up by listening to music.

**terrible**

You look terrible today. Are you sick or something?

The weather is terrible.

He is a terrible person.

**interrupt**

I don't want to get interrupted in the middle of doing something.

He interrupted our conversation.

Who is making this noise? The creaking sound interrupts the class!

**embarrassed**

I was embarrassed when he called out my name loudly on the street.

It's embarrassing to watch a couple kissing in public places.

What was the most embarrassing moment in your life?

**break up**

I broke up with my boyfriend.

I am thinking of breaking up with my boyfriend.

I'm interested in breaking things up.

**yell**

Stop yelling. The baby is sleeping now.

My mom was so furious and started to yell at me.

Well-mannered men never yell.

**scowl**

I stepped on his foot and he scowled at me.

I saw his scowling face in my dream.

I smiled at his scowling face.

mannered

He is bad-mannered.

There are so many bad-mannered people.

Don't you know any manners?

hurry

Let's hurry.

We are in such a hurry.

I hurried into the house.

| **Remember!** | **Write five expressions of your choice.** |
|---|---|
| 1. | |
| 2. | |
| 3. | |
| 4. | |
| 5. | |

## Situation 22 I have to clean up the house!

Laura : Hello, Laura speaking.

Julie : Hi, Laura.
This is Julie and I want to ask you a favor and please don't say no.

Laura : Oh, are you in trouble?

Julie : Yes, and it is huge. I don't know what to do about it.
You are the only person who can save me from this.

Laura : What happened, you trouble maker?

Julie : My parents went on vacation, you know.

Laura : Yeah, to celebrate their $25^{th}$ wedding anniversary.
They went to France, right?

Julie : Yeah, and they were not supposed to come home until next week. And I had a party with my other friends last night. I thought of inviting you but you had this big exam coming up.
So I didn't even tell you about it because I was kind of sorry.

Laura : You had a party last night at your parents' house? Are you insane? Your parents will kill you if they find out about it.

Julie : I know and I got the phone call from my father just now.

Laura : What did he say?

Julie : He said they are arriving home in two hours. He had to cancel the remaining itinerary because of an important meeting.

Laura : Wow, so what do you want from me?

Julie : The house is a mess because I just woke up to answer my father's phone call. I can never clean it up myself within two hours.

Laura : Okay, you need me to clean up the place.
I will hurry to your house though I am doing something important now. I don't want to get you killed by your parents.

Julie : I am so happy to have a friend like you. Thanks a million.

## Say in English!

A: 여보세요, Laura입니다.
B: 안녕 Laura. 나 Julie야.

A: 문제가 생겼니?
B: 응 큰 문제야.

A: 내게 뭘 원하니?
B: 집 청소를 좀 도와줘.

A: 혼자서는 도저히 두 시간 내에 청소할 수 없다니까.
B: 알았어. 집 청소를 해달라는 거지.

## Be brave!

in trouble

Are you in trouble?

Yes, I need your help.

save

Could you save me from my misery?

It might sound cruel but nobody can save you except yourself.

insane

Why did you yell on the street?

I must have been insane.

wake up

What time did you wake up today?

At 7 A.M. as usual.

cancel

What if it rains tomorrow?

We would cancel all our plans.

## Upgrade it!

trouble

I am in trouble. Please help me.

I have trouble reading the book. The letters are too small.

Someone will be there for you when you are in trouble.

cancel

Let's cancel the original plan.

We cancelled the party.

Why did they cancel the order?

mess

The living room is in such a mess.

He can mess up your life. Break up with him.

The room is messy.

huge

I am not hungry because I had a huge breakfast.

He made a huge mistake.

My boyfriend and I had a huge fight last night.

save

You saved my life.

Let's save it for later use.

I saved my face thanks to you.

anniversary

When is your wedding anniversary?

Tomorrow is our 2nd anniversary.

What is good as an anniversary present?

wake

I woke up late this morning?

Wake him up. It's time to go to school.

I want a wake-up call at 6:00 tomorrow.

arrive

What time are they arriving?

He arrived at two in the afternoon.

When I arrived home, it was almost midnight.

remain

What are you going to do during the remaining vacation?

It remains to be seen whether he will keep his word.

I want to remain as your true friend.

celebrate

A lot of people came to my house to celebrate my birthday.

Let's celebrate our love.

I am holding a party to celebrate our reunion.

## Cultural Tip!

**파티의 종류**

미국에서는 파티의 종류도 많다. 미국인들은 어떤 파티들을 즐기며 자신들의 삶을 즐기는지 알아보자.

1. 디너 파티 (dinner party)
   저녁식사 파티이고 격식이 있고 뷔페식으로 열리는 경우가 많다.
2. 칵테일 파티 (cocktail party)
   술과 가벼운 스낵류가 있가 있는 파티이다. 주로 부부 동반으로 열리는 경우가 많다.
3. b.y.o.b (Bring your own booze/bottle)
   각자 자기가 마실 술을 들고 와서 같이 마시는 파티이다.
4. 프람 (prom)
   고등학교 졸업 전에 하는 정장 댄스 파티이다. 반드시 파트너를 동반해서 참석해야 한다.
5. 베이비 샤워 (baby shower)
   출산 직전의 임산부나 태어난 갓난아기를 축하하는 여자들만의 파티이다. 간단한 선물을 준비해서 들고 가는 것이 좋다.
6. 포틀럭 파티 (potluck party)
   각자 자신이 준비한 요리를 들고 와서 함께 먹는 파티이다. 여러 사람이 먹을 수 있는 양을 준비해야 한다.
7. 브라이달 샤워 (bridal shower)
   신부가 될 사람에게 선물을 주기 위하여 여는 다과 파티이다.
8. 하우스 워밍 파티 (housewarming party)

흔히 말하는 집들이 이다. 여러 사람이 북적거리며 새로 이사온 집을 훈훈하게 만든다는 의미에서 나온 말이다.

9. 서프라이즈 파티 (surprise party)

   흔히 말하는 깜짝파티이다. 주인공 몰래 준비해서 놀라게 해주는 것이 특징이다.

10. 파자마 파티 (pajama party)

   보통 10대의 여학생들이 어느 한 친구집에 모여서 잠옷을 입고 같이 수다를 떨고 노는 파티이다. 슬럼버(slumber) 파티라고도 한다.

11. 오픈 하우스 (open house)

   새 집에 이사했을 때, 이웃 사람이나 회사 등의 동료를 초대하여 여는 파티이다. 특정한 시간대를 알려주어 그 시간 안에 언제든지 방문할 수 있는 파티이다.

12. 스태그 파티 (stag party)

   결혼할 친구를 축하하는 독신 남성의 파티를 뜻한다. 여성만의 파티는 'hen party' 라고 한다.

13. 커스텀 파티 (costume party)

   할로윈 경에 열리는 파티로 가장 무도회라 할 수 있다. 여러가지 괴기스러운 분장을 하는 경우가 많다.

14. 추수감사절 파티 (Thanksgiving party)

   미국의 추수감사절에 하는 파티로서 칠면조 고기가 주로 등장한다.

15. 가든 파티 (Garden party)

   뒤뜰이나 정원에서 하는 파티이다.

| **Remember!** | **Write five expressions of your choice.** |
|---|---|
| 1. | |
| 2. | |
| 3. | |
| 4. | |
| 5. | |

## Survive Yourself!

I am going to break up with him.

What happened?

What's going on?

What did you say?

---

I don't want to even think about it.

But you should face the reality.

It's not good to avoid everything.

---

I don't want to see him again.

Did you break up with him?

Something happened between you two, right?

---

It was so horrible!

Well, it was okay with me.

Yeah, you're right.

Was it that horrible?

---

I got a phone call from my father.

What did he say?

You must be happy.

Why did he call you?

---

I am so happy to have a friend like you!

That's what I want to say.

I'm so happy, too.

---

You are the only person who can save me from this.

What are you talking about?

What do you mean?

I don't think so.

Oh, yeah?

---

My parents went on vacation.

Where to?

Wow, they must be excited!

Why not you?

---

Unit 12

# Future Plans

Talk in ENGLISH+

Unit 12

# Future Plans

## Pronounce it!

**Syllabic /n/ 음절 n…**

/n / - /syllabic N/

student kitten button mountain cotton curtain important

garden certain hot and cold bread and butter wouldn't

## Speak out!

Do you know the student?

Have you eaten yet?

Look at the kitten.

Could you press the button?

They are climbing down the mountain.

It's important.

It's hot and cold.

I wouldn't do that.

The garden next door is beautiful.

That little boy looks frightened.

## Tips!

▸ /t/나 /d/음에 강세가 있고 그 뒤 강세 없는 음절이 /n/음에서 끝날 때 /n/음은 음절자음이 된다고 한다. 즉, /n/음은 혀가 입 천장에 닿은 채 발음된다. 발음은 '은'으로 발음하면 된다. 예를 들면, button, kitten, would not have의 경우, '벌-은', '킬-은' , '울-나렵'식으로 발음이 된다.

## Situation 23 I want to run my own business.

Laura : What are you doing?

Julie : You see I am studying.

Laura : What for? The mid term exam just ended. You need a break.

Julie : No, I don't think so. I have to prepare for my future.

Laura : What exactly are you preparing for?

Julie : I want to get a job right after graduation and I have to study very hard because of the cut-throat competition.

Laura: Well, entering a company is not the only way.
Today the weather's just too beautiful to stay indoors. Let's get outside and plan our bright future together in the sun.

Julie : You are so carefree. What are you going to do after graduation if you can't pass the company entrance examination? You know it's hard.

Laura: Yeah, actually it's too hard for me and I gave it up already.

Julie : What are you talking about? My mother would kill me if I couldn't get a job after graduation.

Laura : I am going to run my own business. If you are interested I can show you some of my business plans. They are not complete yet, but it will be very intriguing.

Julie : Really? Why didn't you tell me anything about them yet?
Of course I am interested. Tell me about it.

Laura : I am not going to tell you here in this stuffy library. Pack your bags and follow me outdoors. After you hear, you will probably beg me to include you in my future business.

Julie : What makes you so confident?

Laura : Well, you will see when you hear my plans. Let's go!

Julie : Okay, it won't hurt. Anyway, I have nothing to lose.

Laura : Nothing to lose? Come on, trust me. You have everything to gain.

## Say in English!

A: 뭐 하고 있어?
B: 공부하고 있잖아.

A: 졸업 후 뭘 할거니?
B: 내 사업을 할 거야.

A: 왜 진작 이야기하지 않았어?
B: 여기 숨막히는 도서관 속에서는 얘기 안 할거야.

A: 왜 그리 자신만만하니?
B: 들어보면 알 거야.

## Be brave!

graduation

Congratulations on your graduation.

Thanks a lot.

stuffy

It's stuffy in here. Would you mind if I open the window?

No, not at all.

pack

Will you help me pack my stuff?

Sure, but I am available during the weekend.

confident

What makes you so confident?

Well, I have a reliable backup plan.

probably

Who is making noise there?

That's probably Tom.

## Upgrade it!

confident

I am confident that I will win the race.

Be confident.

You are overly confident.

graduation

After graduation, I will enter a company.

What are you going to do after graduation?

When is the graduation ceremony?

break

Give me a break!

We'll have a coffee break for thirty minutes.

Let's have a cigarette break for ten minutes and continue.

stuffy

The room is stuffy. Open the window.

Isn't it stuffy in here?

I have a stuffy nose because of my cold.

competition

Competition is fierce these days.

There was less competition in the past.

I need some information on the competition.

outdoors

I enjoy playing sports outdoors.

Let's enjoy the weather outdoors.

entrance

Where is the entrance gate?

When is the college entrance examination?

Entrance is free.

job

That's not my job.

What kind of job would you like to have?

I've got a new job.

trust

Do you trust me?

Trust me.

We need some time to build trust between ourselves.

gain

I need to gain some weight.

Gain some points after you fill out the survey form.

No pains, no gains.

complete

Complete the mission please.

My job is complete now.

It requires complete devotion.

## Cultural Tip!

**미국의 의식주 문화**

**의**

한국에서 인기 있는 미국 브랜드 상품들도 물론 미국에서 인기 있다. 하지만 미국사람들은 그리 부자가 아니라면 좀 가진 사람이라 해도 절약하며 사는 사람들이 많다. 그래서 의복에 그리 많은 돈을 쓰지는 않는다. 물론 패션 리더며 많은 멋쟁이 들이 많기도 한 나라가 미국이기도 하지만, 아이러니하게도 자기 개성에 맞게 입고 다니는 사람들도 많다. 또한 직접 옷을 만들어 입거나 뜨개질로 만들 조끼나 니트들을 즐겨 입기도 한다. 또한 메이커 옷을 저렴하게 파는 초대형 outlet 매장들도 많이 볼 수 있다.

**식**

많은 미국인들은 캔 음료나 패스트푸드를 즐겨 먹는 편이다. 물론 요즘엔 건강에 신경을 쓰는 사람들이 늘어나서 외식하는 비용으로 개인 영양사를 채용해서 식단 짜주는 것으로 칼로리 조절 하는 사람도 있기도 하다. 미국은 외식비가 비싼 편이기는 하지만 여전히 외식을 즐기는 사람들이 많다. 미국사람들은 소다를 좋아하는 사람들이 많은데 소다나 다른 음료를 취향대로 하나만 고집하며 마시는 마니아 층 사람들이 많다. 예를 들어서 코카콜라를 마시는 사람은 웬만하면 펩시콜라를 마시지 않고 그 반대도 마찬가지이다.

**주**

대개 미국인들은 single house를 가지기도 하지만, multi family house (여러 가정이 사는 집-

집주인이 세를 주는 형태로 주인이 2~3가정에게 세를 주는 형태)와 condominium (콘도 - 콘도는 대개 자기 집처럼 분양 받을 수 있는 형태)에 사는 사람들도 많이 있다. 단 그 콘도 회사에 의해 약간의 간섭을 받을 수 있다. 여러 가정들이 콘도 안에 함께 살기 때문에 예를 들어 콘도 내에선 금연이라든지 동물을 키울 수 없다든지, 자신들의 마당에 식물을 함부로 심을 수 없다든지 하는 좀 까다로운 곳도 있다. 그리고 duplex house라는 주택 형태는 대개 주택을 대칭모양으로 지어서 중간을 막고 두 가정이 사는 형태로 자신의 집처럼 분양 받을 수 있다. 단층 내지 2층의 구조로 되어 있는 경우가 많다. 그 외에 아파트에 세를 얻어 사는 경우가 있는데 미국에서는 아파트는 분양 받을 수 있는 형태로 되어있지 세를 놓는 형태로 되어 있는 경우가 많다.

| **Remember!** | **Write five expressions of your choice.** |
|---|---|
| 1. | |
| 2. | |
| 3. | |
| 4. | |
| 5. | |

## Situation 24 You are a promising young man.

Professor : I saw your proposal for the final term paper. I liked that idea very much.

Kevin : Thank you, Dr. Holt.

Professor : Where did you get the idea?

Kevin : Actually I have been thinking of it for a long time.
I am going to open my own business based on the idea.

Professor : Oh, really? It means you thought about the details of the plan already?

Kevin : Yes, and I have done much of the market research as well.

Professor : Brilliant! I am very curious. Are you going to give me more detailed presentation of your plans?

Kevin : Of course if you are interested.
But now I have to hurry to my accounting class.

Professor : What about tomorrow at two? Meet me at my office.
There is a national contest for business plans and only college students are eligible. With a little help, you have a good chance of winning, I am sure.

Kevin : Wow, I am excited. Tomorrow at two would be fine.
As a matter of fact, I always wanted to discuss it with someone who has more knowledge and experience.

Professor : Well then, see you tomorrow. Prepare some more documents to back up your ideas.

Kevin : Don't worry about it, ma'am. I have lots of them.

Professor : You are a promising young man.
You will surely make an excellent entrepreneur.

Kevin : Do you really think so? Thank you, ma'am. I'm so flattered. I will be all ready for tomorrow's presentation. I won't disappoint you.

Professor : You've already proven yourself. Don't overwork yourself.
Let's discuss it together over tea and make some improvements.

Kevin : All right, Dr. Holt. See you tomorrow and have a nice day.

Professor : Bye.

## Say in English!

A: 어디서 아이디어를 얻었는가?

B: 사실은 오랫동안 생각해왔던 것입니다.

A: 너의 아이디어를 뒷받침해줄 자료를 좀 준비해 오게나.

B: 걱정하지 마세요. 많이 있습니다.

A: 내일 두 시면 어떤가?

B: 내일 두 시 좋습니다.

A: 이미 자네의 능력을 증명했으니 너무 지나치게 열심히 하지는 말게나.

B: 네, Holt 박사님. 내일 뵙겠습니다. 좋은 하루 보내세요.

## Be brave!

promising

Why do you think he is promising?

First of all, he is diligent.

based on

Why do you say to me such a thing?

Based on what I heard from Jane.

entrepreneur

His sense of business is great.

Yeah, I think so, too. He will be a remarkable entrepreneur.

discuss

Who do you discuss the matter with?

I usually talk with my lawyer.

hurry

Why do we have to hurry?

Because of the traffic jam.

## Upgrade it!

open

I opened the book.

The gate is open.

Open sesame!

curious

Aren't you curious about the results?

She has always been the curious type.

Curiosity killed the cat.

make

You will make a good husband.

You will make a good teacher.

He will make it.

discuss

Let's discuss it over lunch.

They discussed the matter at length.

Let's discuss it later.

disappointed

Are you disappointed?

Nothing disappoints me.

Did I disappoint you?

prepare

Let's prepare for the interview.

My mom is preparing lunch.

Are you preparing for the test?

flatter

You flattered me.

I am so flattered.

It is very flattering.

worry

Don't worry. Be happy.

I am worried about you.

I am not worried at all.

excellent

You are an excellent student.

The test results are excellent.

What is so excellent about his report?

prove

Can you prove that you are loyal?

He proved himself to be faithful.

Can you prove that God exists?

chance

Chances are slim.

There is a good chance that you will win the game.

I don't want to take any chances.

| **Remember!** | **Write five expressions of your choice.** |
| --- | --- |
| 1. | |
| 2. | |
| 3. | |
| 4. | |
| 5. | |

## Survive Yourself!

You have everything to gain.

Are you really sure about that?

Can I trust you?

Well, if you say so.

---

I have nothing to lose.

So, what are you gonna do now?

What's your next choice?

What do you mean?

---

They are not complete yet.

Not yet?

When is it supposed to be completed?

How long do you think it will take?

---

Hearing it won't hurt.

That's right.

So, you are gonna go?

---

You have a good chance of winning.

Do you really think so?

I'm not sure.

That's what I hope.

---

What about tomorrow at two?

Tomorrow at two?

Hmm, it's a little too late. How about one?

Ok, tomorrow at two sharp.

Well, I'm not sure.

---

You will surely make an excellent entrepreneur.

Thank you for saying so.

Thanks.

I have a great aim for my future.

---

You are a promising young man.

Thank you.

Thanks. I will do my best.

---

# 단어카드

Talk in **ENGLISH+**

| | |
|---|---|
| Unit 1<br>Is this seat taken? | Unit 1<br>Never mind. |
| Unit 1<br>Are you from around here? | Unit 1<br>Did you do anything special over the vacation? |
| Unit 1<br>Daegu is famous for its apples. | Unit 1<br>Long time, no see. |
| Unit 1<br>You must be kidding! | Unit 1<br>What's up? |
| Unit 1<br>I've never heard of that before. | Unit 1<br>Have you ever been there? |
| Unit 1<br>I'm in my first year. | Unit 1<br>I'm thinking about going abroad next year. |

신경 쓰지마.

/mind 신경 쓰다, 마음에 두다

이 자리에 앉아도 되나요?

/seat 자리 taken (자리 등이) 차지된

방학 때 뭐 특별히 한 일 있어?

/anything special 뭔가 특별한 것, over (기간에) 걸쳐서,

이곳 출신이세요?

/from ~출신의,

오랜만이야

대구는 사과로 유명해.

/is famous for ~로 유명한

무슨 일이야?

농담이시죠!

/kidding 농담 must be ~틀림없어

그 곳에 가본 적 있니?

/have been 가본적 있는

예전에 들어본 적이 없는데요.

/never heard 결코 들어보지 못하다

난 내년에 해외에 가볼까 생각 중입니다.

/think about ~대해 생각하다, go aboard 해외로 가다

전 1학년입니다.

/first year 1학년인

Unit 2

I'll have a large coffee.

Unit 2

Is there anything wrong?

Unit 2

Can you get some cream and sugar for me?

Unit 2

I don't wanna spoil my friendship.

Unit 2

You have my word.

Unit 2

Can I get you anything to drink?

Unit 2

I'll give him a call later.

Unit 2

Is there any fun?

Unit 2

What's that supposed to mean?

Unit 2

How would you like that?

Unit 2

I mean it.

Unit 2

I'll be right back.

뭐 잘못된 것 있어?

/wrong 잘못된

커피 큰 걸로 주세요.

/have(=drink, eat)

우정을 망치고 싶지 않아.

/spoil 망치다

크림이랑 설탕 좀 갖다 줄래?

/ get some 좀 가져다 주다.

마실 것 좀 갖다 드릴까요?

/get (someone) anything - 좀 갖다 주다.

약속할게.

재미는 있니?

/fun 재미

그에게 나중에 전화해야겠어.

/give a call 전화하다. 전화 걸다

어떻게 해서 드시겠어요?

/would like - 하고 싶다

무슨 뜻으로 하는 말이야?

/be supposed to - 하기로 되어있다.

곧 돌아올게.

/be back(=get back)

정말이야.

/mean 뜻하다.

Unit 3

Which movie do you want to see?

Unit 3

I don't know what to say.

Unit 3

I heard that movie is well made.

Unit 3

Don't grumble about it.

Unit 3

Who is starring in the movie?

Unit 3

There is no alternative.

Unit 3

You won't regret it.

Unit 3

What do you want to see?

Unit 3

Enjoy the movie.

Unit 3

Don't flatter me!

Unit 3

What's playing?

Unit 3

I'm so lucky to have a friend like you.

뭐라 해야 할 지 모르겠어.
/what to say 무슨 말을 해야 할지

무슨 영화 보고 싶어?

칭얼거리지 마.
/grumble 투덜거리다.

그 영화 잘 만들었다던데.
/well made 잘 만들어진

선택의 여지가 없어.
/alternative 양자택일, 선택

그 영화에 누가 나오니?
/starring 출연하는

뭐 보고 싶어?

후회 안 할거야.
/won't(=will not), regret 후회하다.

아부 그만해.
/flatter 아부하다

영화 잘 봐.
/enjoy 즐기다

너 같은 친구를 둬서 행운이야.
/like - 같은, lucky 행운인, 운 좋은

무슨 영화가 상영되니?
/play 상영하다, 공연하다

| | |
|---|---|
| Unit 4<br>I'd like to have a boyfriend (girlfriend). | Unit 4<br>Don't brag about me too much. |
| Unit 4<br>What does he look like? | Unit 4<br>How did your date go? |
| Unit 4<br>I can set you up with my best friend. | Unit 4<br>How embarrassing! |
| Unit 4<br>What's he like? | Unit 4<br>I hope you guys get along well. |
| Unit 4<br>He can be a little stubborn. | Unit 4<br>That's ridiculous. |
| Unit 4<br>Let me check my schedule. | Unit 4<br>What's that supposed to mean? |

| | |
|---|---|
| 내 자랑 너무 하지마.<br>/brag 자랑하다, too much 너무 | 남자친구(여자친구) 있으면 좋겠다.<br>/I'd like to - 하고 싶다 |
| 데이트 어땠어? | 어떻게 생겼어?<br>/look like - 처럼 보이다 |
| 저런 난처한 일이!<br>/embarrassing 당황스러운 | 내 친한 친구 소개시켜 줄게.<br>/set up 소개시켜 주다. |
| 너희들 잘 되었으면 좋겠어.<br>/get along well 잘 지내다 | 성격은 어때? |
| 말도 안돼.<br>/ridiculous 어리석은 | 약간 고집이 세.<br>/stubborn 고집 센 |
| 그게 무슨 뜻이야? | 내 스케줄 좀 확인해 볼게.<br>/let me - 할게. |

| | |
|---|---|
| Unit 5<br>I'm really depressed these days. | Unit 5<br>I feel much better now. |
| Unit 5<br>You broke up with your boyfriend? | Unit 5<br>You look more human. |
| Unit 5<br>I am so over him! | Unit 5<br>I lost my appetite. |
| Unit 5<br>I don't have any feelings for him at all. | Unit 5<br>Why don't you take a break? |
| Unit 5<br>He looks perfect. | Unit 5<br>What's that thing on your shirt? |
| Unit 5<br>What's got into you? | Unit 5<br>I'm not myself today. |

| | |
|---|---|
| **기분이 훨씬 좋아졌어.**<br>/feel better 기분이 좋아지다. | **요즘 너무 우울해.**<br>/depressed 우울해 these days 요즘 |
| **너 더 인간적으로 보여.**<br>/look human 인간적으로 보이다. | **남자친구랑 헤어졌다고?**<br>/break up with 헤어지다 |
| **식욕을 잃었어.**<br>/lose appetite 식욕을 잃다 | **그를 깨끗이 잊었다니까!**<br>/over someone -를 극복하다, 다 잊다 |
| **좀 쉬는 게 어때?**<br>/why don't you? 어때?, take a break 휴식을 취하다 | **아무런 감정도 남아 있지 않아.**<br>/not at all 전혀 아니다. |
| **셔츠에 묻은 게 그게 뭐야?**<br>/that thing 그것, 그 물건 | **그는 완벽해 보여.**<br>/look 보이다 |
| **오늘 제 정신이 아니야**<br>/not myself 제 정신이 아닌 | **너 도대체 왜 그러니?**<br>/get into 들어가다. 스며들다 |

| | |
|---|---|
| Unit 6<br>You can say that again. | Unit 6<br>I'll carry this one with me. |
| Unit 6<br>Where's the check in counter? | Unit 6<br>This is my first time to take an international flight. |
| Unit 6<br>Isn't it better to wait for Mark? | Unit 6<br>When do they serve lunch? |
| Unit 6<br>I just got his message. | Unit 6<br>My stomach is rumbling. |
| Unit 6<br>Is it the direct flight to Vancouver? | Unit 6<br>Don't forget to fill in your immigration card. |
| Unit 6<br>I can hang around Tokyo. | Unit 6<br>She's well prepared. |

이건 기내에 들고 탈 거야.

/carry 운반하다, 들다

두말하면 잔소리지!

국제선은 처음 타는 거야.

/international flight 국제선

체크 인 카운터가 어디지?

/check in counter 입출국수속대

점심 언제 주니?

/serve lunch 점심을 제공하다

Mark를 기다리는 게 더 낫지 않아?

/wait for 기다리다

위장에서 천둥소리가 나.

/stomach 위 rumbling 으르렁거리다

방금 메시지 받았어.

/get a message 메시지 받다

입국카드 작성하는 것 잊지마.

/immigration card 입국카드
fill in 작성하다

벤쿠버까지 직항이니?

/direct flight 직항

그녀는 항상 준비가 철저해.

/well prepared 준비가 잘 된

도쿄 구경을 좀 해야지.

/hang around 구경다니다. 돌아다니다

| | |
|---|---|
| Unit 7<br>Where is the best place to look around? | Unit 7<br>You can see it on the map here. |
| Unit 7<br>Do you want to join me? | Unit 7<br>How many shows do they have tonight? |
| Unit 7<br>He just stepped out. | Unit 7<br>It's our turn. |
| Unit 7<br>Let's drop by the Visitor's Center first. | Unit 7<br>Do you have tickets for the 7 o'clock show? |
| Unit 7<br>Can I get a map of this city? | Unit 7<br>We still have 3 more hours left. |
| Unit 7<br>You've been here in Vancouver, right? | Unit 7<br>I'm going on a camping trip. |

| | |
|---|---|
| **여기 지도상에 나와있네요.**<br>/on the map 지도상에 | **구경 다니기 좋은 곳이 어디죠?**<br>/look around 둘러보다, 구경하다 |
| **오늘밤 몇 차례 상영 하나요?**<br>/shows 상영 | **나랑 함께 갈래?**<br>/join함께 가다. |
| **우리 차례야.**<br>/our turn 우리 차례 | **그는 방금 나갔어.**<br>/step out 나가다 |
| **7시 쇼 티켓이 있습니까?** | **여행자 센터에 먼저 들르자.**<br>/drop by 들르다, Visitor's Center 여행자센터 |
| **우리 아직 세 시간이나 더 남았어.**<br>/3 more hours 세시간 더 | **이 도시 지도 좀 얻을 수 있을까요?**<br>/get a map 지도를 구하다 |
| **난 캠핑 갈거야.**<br>/go on a camping trip 캠핑가다 | **너 예전에 벤쿠버 와봤었지?** |

Unit 8

How can I get to Starry Park?

Unit 8

Can I ask you something?

Unit 8

Let me ask.

Unit 8

Can you show me where I am on this map?

Unit 8

We should go this way.

Unit 8

I'm looking for the Central Theater.

Unit 8

The map says we should turn right.

Unit 8

I'm not from here myself.

Unit 8

Why don't we walk a little more?

Unit 8

Excuse me, I need some help.

Unit 8

I'm really expecting it.

Unit 8

My pleasure.

뭐 좀 물어봐도 돼?

/ask something 뭔가 물어보다

스타리 공원까지 어떻게 갑니까?

/get to - 에 가다, 도착하다

이 지도상에서 제 위치를 말씀해 주시겠어요?

/show me 알려주다
where I am 여기가 어디인지

내가 물어볼게.

센트럴 극장을 찾고 있는데요.

/look for -을 찾다

이 쪽으로 가야 해.

/this way 이쪽

저도 이 곳 출신이 아니라서요.

/from here 이곳 출신인

지도에서는 우회전해야 한다고 되어있어.

/turn right 우회전하다

실례합니다. 도움이 좀 필요한데요.

조금만 더 걸어갈래?

/a little more 조금 더

별 말씀을.

/pleasure 기쁨, 즐거움

정말 기대되는걸.

/expect 기대하다

| | |
|---|---|
| Unit 9<br>How have you been? | Unit 9<br>He must make good money. |
| Unit 9<br>You look different. | Unit 9<br>I've been really busy. |
| Unit 9<br>It is outdated now. | Unit 9<br>I have no personal life now. |
| Unit 9<br>You look the same. | Unit 9<br>That makes sense. |
| Unit 9<br>Did you lose some weight? | Unit 9<br>He is so demanding. |
| Unit 9<br>I can recommend someone for you. | Unit 9<br>Don't blame yourself. |

| | |
|---|---|
| 돈 정말 잘 벌겠네.<br>/make money 돈 벌다 | 어떻게 지냈어? |
| 정말 바빴었어. | 너 좀 달라 보인다. |
| 난 사생활이 없어.<br>/personal life 사생활 | 그건 이제 한물갔는걸.<br>/outdated 구식인, 뒤떨어진 |
| 그거 말 되네.<br>/make sense 일리가 있는, 말되는 | 뭐 똑같아 보이는데.<br>/the same 똑 같은 |
| 그는 너무 까다로워.<br>/demanding 요구가 많은, 까다로운 | 살은 좀 빠졌니?<br>/lose weight 살 빠지다 |
| 너무 자책하지마.<br>/blame 비난하다, 책망하다 | 내가 누군가 추천해 줄 수 있는데.<br>/recommend 추천하다 |

| | |
|---|---|
| Unit 10<br>Are you free this afternoon? | Unit 10<br>Can I speak to Julie, please? |
| Unit 10<br>What do you want from me? | Unit 10<br>This is me, Julie. |
| Unit 10<br>My parents' wedding anniversary is coming up. | Unit 10<br>Something big is up. |
| Unit 10<br>It won't take long. | Unit 10<br>Tell me about the details. |
| Unit 10<br>We have plenty of time. | Unit 10<br>It's not like him. |
| Unit 10<br>I don't want to miss the 7:30 show. | Unit 10<br>I'm so envious of you guys. |

| | |
|---|---|
| **Julie와 통화할 수 있을까요?**<br>/speak to -와 통화하다 | **오늘 오후에 시간 있어?**<br>/free 한가한, 여유 있는 |
| **(전화통화) 나 Julie야.**<br>/this is(전화통화) 저는 입니다. | **내게 원하는 게 뭐야?** |
| **큰 일이 생겼어.**<br>/something big 뭔가 큰 일 | **우리 부모님 결혼기념일이 다가오고 있어.**<br>/anniversary 기념일, coming up 다가오는 |
| **자세히 좀 말해봐.**<br>/details 세부사항, 자세한 사항 | **오래 걸리진 않을 거야.**<br>/take (시간)걸리다 |
| **평소의 그답지 않네.**<br>/like 같은, 처럼 | **시간은 충분해.**<br>/plenty of 충분한 |
| **너희들 정말 부럽다.**<br>/envious 부러워하는 | **7시30분 프로는 놓치고 싶지않아.**<br>/miss 놓치다, 잃어버리다 |

| | |
|---|---|
| Unit 11<br>Is anything wrong? | Unit 11<br>I want to ask you a favor. |
| Unit 11<br>He asked me to go out for dinner. | Unit 11<br>Are you in trouble? |
| Unit 11<br>I didn't want to get interrupted. | Unit 11<br>Are you insane? |
| Unit 11<br>I was so embarrassed. | Unit 11<br>Thanks a million. |
| Unit 11<br>I totally agree with you. | Unit 11<br>You know. |
| Unit 11<br>Calm down. | Unit 11<br>My house is a mess. |

네게 부탁하고 싶은 게 하나 있는데.

/ask a favor 부탁하다

뭐 안 좋은 일이라도 있어?

뭐 문제라도 있어?

/in trouble 곤경에 처한, 문제가 있는

그가 저녁식사 하러 가자고 하던데.

너 제정신이야?

/insane 제 정신이 아닌, 미친

방해 받고 싶지 않았어.

/get interrupted 방해 받다

너무 고마워.

나 너무 당황했어.

/embarrassed 당황한

너도 알다시피

나도 전적으로 너와 같은 생각이야.

/agree with 동의하다, totally 전적으로

집이 엉망이야.

/mess 엉망, 헝클어짐, 뒤죽박죽

진정해.

/calm 차분한, 고요한

| | |
|---|---|
| Unit 12<br>I want to run my own business. | Unit 12<br>I have nothing to lose. |
| Unit 12<br>You see I am studying? | Unit 12<br>Trust me. |
| Unit 12<br>Let's get outside. | Unit 12<br>I am very curious. |
| Unit 12<br>You are so carefree. | Unit 12<br>Meet me at my office. |
| Unit 12<br>I gave it up already. | Unit 12<br>Tomorrow at two would be fine. |
| Unit 12<br>What makes you so confident? | Unit 12<br>I'm so flattered. |

손해 볼 거 없어.

/lose 잃어버리다

내 사업을 하고 싶어.

/run a business 사업을 하다

나만 믿어

/trust 믿다, 신뢰하다

공부하는 거 안 보여?

궁금한 걸.

/curious 호기심에 찬, 궁금한

밖으로 나가자.

/get outside 밖으로 나가다

내 사무실에서 만나자.

/meet me 만나자

넌 정말 태평이구나.

/carefree 태평인, 느긋한

내일 두 시 좋아요.

난 벌써 포기했어.

/give up 포기하다

우쭐해 지는데요.

/flattered 우쭐해 하는

왜 그렇게 자신만만하니?

/confident 자신감이 넘치는

Script

# Say in English!

Talk in **ENGLISH+**

## Unit 01 School Life

### Situation 1 Meeting Someone New

**Say in English!**

A: Is this seat taken?
B: Not at all.

A: I grew up here. You?
B: I'm from Busan.

A: What do you mean by "women"?
B: People say there are a lot of attractive women in Daegu.

A: Let's hope for the best and prepare for the worst just in case.
B: Alright.

### Situation 2 What's up?

**Say in English!**

A: Hey Rachel, long time, no see.
B: Hi Julie. Good to see you.

A: I went to Thailand for a couple of weeks.
B: I went there last year.

A: I'm thinking about going abroad next year to study English.
B: There are a lot of places to study here in Korea

A: It sounds like you have thought a lot about this. Good luck.
B: Thanks.

## Unit 02 Café & Restaurant

### Situation 3 At a Café

**Say in English!**

A: How can I help you?
B: I'll have a large coffee.

A: Can you get some cream and sugar for me?
B: Sure.

A: Have you seen the Herman Hesse exhibition at Busan Museum?

B: Yes, I went last weekend.
A: People say you guys are going out together a lot recently.
B: I'm not going out with him a lot. I mean it!

### Situation 4 At a Restaurant

**Say in English!**

A: Do you have a table next to the window?
B: How is this?

A: Can I get you anything to drink?
B: I'd like a lemonade.

A: It's been a long time since we came here.
B: Yeah, it's a long time.

A: How's your school life? Is there any fun?
B: It's just great.

## Unit 03 Movies

### Situation 5 At the movies

**Say in English!**

A: Which movie do you want to see?
B: I heard Ocean's 15 is great.

A: Do you want something to eat?
B: That's a good idea.

A: Did you see Ocean's 14?
B: I've seen all the series.

A: I think I should rent the DVD.
B: That's your call, but you won't regret it.

### Situation 6 What's playing?

**Say in English!**

A: Do you want to see a movie tonight?
B: Hmm. Maybe. What's playing?

A: I'm interested in the new Halle Berry movie.
B: Hmm. I personally don't like Halle Berry.

A: I heard that movie is well made and it makes us think.
B: I don't know what to say. I particularly don't like Japanese movies.

A: I'm so lucky to have a friend like you.
B: Don't flatter me!

## Unit 04 Dating

### Situation 7 Set me up!

**Say in English!**

A: What does he look like?
B: He's kind of tall and very good looking.

A: What's he like?
B: He's charming and has a great sense of humor.

A: Then how about next Wednesday after school?
B: That sounds fine with me.

A: Don't brag about me too much.
B: No worries.

### Situation 8 How did Your Date Go?

**Say in English!**

A: Tell me about your date last night.
B: It was good at first.

A: I had money, but he insisted that he should pay.
B: That's ridiculous.

A: Other than the dinner incident, he was very nice, kind, and even very funny.
B: Good to hear that.

A: I hope you guys get along well.
B: Thanks for your concern.

## Unit 05 Feeling

### Situation 9 I need to be refreshed.

**Say in English!**

A: Hey, what's up?
B: I'm really depressed.

A: I just think I am missing something important in my life.
B: You know where I am, if you need me.

A: I think she chose him because he's rich
B: What's got into you?

A: Thanks. I feel much better now.
B: Don't mention it.

### Situation 10 You look more human.

**Say in English!**

A: Why don't you take a break?
B: I have to finish this today.

A: Do you want some chocolate?
B: I'll just have a cup of tea then.

A: You work too much.
B: Do you think it's a problem?

A: What's that thing on your shirt?
B: Gee… it's coffee!

## Unit 06 Airport

### Situation11 This airport is crowded.

**Say in English!**

A: Where's the check in counter?
B: It's right over there.

A: Isn't it better to wait for Mark?
B: He said he would be at the airport sometime soon.

A: Is it the direct flight?
B: We're gonna stop in Tokyo and transfer to the connecting flight.

A: You just have two bags?
B: Do you have three bags to check in?

### Situation 12 In flight

**Say in English!**

A: This is my first time to take an international flight.
B: It's almost the same as a domestic flight.

A: When do they serve lunch?
B: In a minute, I guess.

A: Anything to drink?
B: Yes, some red wine, please.

A: With or without gas?
B: Without, please.

## Unit 07 Travel

### Situation 13 There are many attractions in this

**Say in English!**

A: Do you want to join me?
B: Sure, but what about Mike?

A: Where is the best place to look around?
B: Let's drop by the Visitor's Center first.

A: You've been here before, right?
B: Yes, but it was long ago.

A: Can I get a map of this city?
B: Sure. Here it is.

### Situation 14 I'd like to reserve tickets.

**Say in English!**

A: How many shows do they have tonight?
B: There are shows at 7:00 and at 9:00.

A: Why don't we reserve tickets for this Saturday?
B: That's a good idea.

A: Are there any good tourist sites near here?
B: How about Starry Park?

A: I'll pay by cash.
B: All right.

## Unit 08 Direction

### Situation15 Turn right at the end of the street.

**Say in English!**

A: Will you take a walk to Starry Park?
B: That's good.

A: How can I get to Starry Park from here?
B: It's not far.

A: You mean that place over there?
B: There it is.

A: It's perfect weather to ride a bike.
B: Yeah, I'm really expecting it.

### Situation 16 Can you show me where I am?

**Say in English!**

A: Can I ask you something?
B: Sure.

A: I'm lost
B: You're on the corner of Main Street and Park Avenue.

A: Can you show me where I am on this map?
B: Now you are here at this point on the map.

A: I've heard it's somewhere around here.
B: I'm not from here myself, either.

## Unit 09 Health & Diet

### Situation 17 I am on a diet.

**Say in English!**

A: How have you been?

B: I've been busy

A: You look different.

B: I lost five kilos.

A: Did you lose some weight?

B: I just started it yesterday.

A: How long are you going to do that?

B: For about a month maybe.

A: Call him right away!

B: I'll do that.

### Situation 18 My father's so demanding!

**Say in English!**

A: Did you call the guy?

B: No, I couldn't.

A: What's up with your father?

B: He sprained his ankle.

A: Is he okay now?

B: He is getting better and better every day.

A: Don't blame yourself.

B: Well, I am not so sure, though.

## Unit 10 Events

### Situation19 My parents' wedding anniversary is coming up!

**Say in English!**

A: Are you free this afternoon?

B: I have no special plans yet. Why do you ask?

A: What do you want from me?

B: Come with me to the department store.

A: So what are you thinking of buying for your parents?

B: A scarf for my mom and a tie for my dad.

A: I'm so glad to have a friend like you.

B: Just call me whenever you need help.

### Situation 20 I'm getting engaged!

**Say in English!**

A: What's up?

B: Something big is up.

A: When did it happen?

B: An hour ago.

A: Isn't it so romantic?

B: It's not like him.

A: Is there another guy?

B: Mark is the only guy for me.

## Unit 11 Trouble

### Situation 21 I had a fight with my boyfriend!

**Say in English!**

A: What do you think?

B: I totally agree with you.

A: What are you going to do now?

B: I am going to break up with him.

A: Is anything wrong?

B: I had a fight with my boyfriend.

A: Calm down and go see a movie or something for a change of air.

B: I want to, but I can't. I have to study.

### Situation 22 I have to clean up the house!

**Say in English!**

A: Hello, Laura speaking.

B: Hi, Laura. This is Julie.

A: Are you in trouble?

B: Yes, and it is huge.

A: What do you want from me?

B: I need your help to clean up the place.

A: I can never clean it up myself within two hours.

B: Okay, you need me to clean up the place.

## Unit 12 Future Plans

### Situation 23 I want to run my own business.

**Say in English!**

A: What are you doing?

B: You see I am studying.

A: What are you going to do after graduation?

B: I am going to run my own business.

A: Why didn't you tell me anything about them yet?

B: I am not going to tell you here in this stuffy library.

A: What makes you so confident?

B: You will see when you hear it.

### Situation 24 You are a promising young man.

**Say in English!**

A: Where did you get the idea?

B: Actually I have been thinking of it for a long time.

A: Prepare some more documents to back up your ideas.

B: Don't worry about it. I have lots of them.

A: What about tomorrow at two?

B: Tomorrow at two would be fine.

A: You've already proven yourself. Don't overwork yourself.

B: All right, Dr. Holt. See you tomorrow and have a nice day.

해석본

# Talk in English +

Talk in ENGLISH +

## Unit 01 School Life

### Situation 1 Meeting Someone New

### 새로운 사람 만나기

Mike: Hi, is this seat taken?
이 자리에 앉아도 되나요?

Kevin: Not at all. Were you in Professor Holt's class last semester?
그럼요, 지난 학기 Holt 교수님 수업 들으셨죠?

Mike: No, my professor was Ms. Stone.
아니요. Stone 교수님 수업 들었어요.
I'm Mike, by the way. What's your name?
그건 그렇고 전 마이크라고 해요. 그쪽은 이름이?

Kevin: Kevin. Nice to meet you, Mike.
전 캐빈입니다. 마이크, 만나서 반가워요.
Are you also a freshman?
당신도 1학년입니까?

Mike: No, I'm a sophomore. Are you from around here?
아니요, 2학년이에요. 이 지역 출신이신가요?

Kevin: Yes, I grew up here. You?
네 여기서 자랐어요. 당신은?

Mike: I'm from Daegu.
저는 대구가 고향입니다.

Kevin: Really? I heard that Daegu is famous for its apples.
정말입니까? 대구는 사과로 유명하다고 들었는데.

Mike: It's not only famous for its apples but also women.
사과뿐만 아니라 여자로도 유명해요.

Kevin: What do you mean by women?
여자라고요? 무슨 뜻이예요?

Mike: People say that there are a lot of attractive women in Daegu.
대구에는 매력적인 여자들이 많다고들 하지요.

Kevin: Really? I've never heard of that before! I think you could set me up with one of them.
정말이에요? 한 번도 들어본 적이 없는데요. 제게 한 사람 소개시켜 주시면 되겠네요.

Mike: You must be kidding! 농담이시죠!!

Kevin: Never mind.
그럼 농담이지요.
Anyway, I hope this class is going to be interesting.
어쨌든 이 수업이 재미있기를 바래요.

Mike: Some of my friends who took this class before said that it was very interesting and worth taking.
이 수업을 이전에 들었던 내 친구들이 수업이 매우 재미있고 들을 만 했다고 하던데요.

Kevin: I'm glad to hear that. 그럼 다행이군요.

Mike: Let's hope for the best and prepare for the worst just in case.
재미있을 거예요. 근데 혹시 모르니까 최악의 경우를 대비합시다.

Kevin: Alright. 좋아요.

### Upgrade it!

He's my professor.
그는 나의 교수님이다.
The professor is from Mexico.
그 교수님은 멕시코인입니다.
My father is a professor.
저의 아버지는 교수님입니다.

How many courses are you taking this semester?
이번 학기에 몇 과목을 듣습니까?
We offer a semester-long study program in Canada.
저희들은 캐나다에서 한 학기 동안 학습할 수 있는 프로그램을 제공합니다.
I teach one semester a year.
저는 일년에 한 학기 가르칩니다.

What is the second thing to do?
두 번째로 해야 할 일이 무엇입니까?
Just give me a second.
잠깐만 시간을 주세요.
On second thought, I don't know why I did that.
다시 한번 생각해보니 내가 왜 그렇게 했는지 모르겠네요.

He is a famous player.
그는 유명한 선수입니다.
I want to become famous.
저는 유명해지고 싶습니다.
I'm not that famous.
저는 그다지 유명하지 않습니다.

She looks really attractive.
그녀는 정말 매력적으로 보입니다.

How attractive she is!
정말 그녀는 매력적이다.
To me, she is the most attractive person in the world.
내게 그녀는 세상에서 가장 매력적인 사람이다.

I've never done that.
나는 절대 그러지 않았어요.
That never occurred to me.
그런 생각이 전혀 들지 않았어요.
Never say that again.
그런 말 다시는 하지 마시오.

The novel is really interesting.
그 소설은 정말 재미있다.
He is an interesting person.
그는 재미있는 사람이다.
Do you want something interesting?
뭔가 흥미로운 것을 원하십니까?

I'm glad you are here.
당신이 여기 있어 좋습니다.
He's glad that his son is safe.
그는 그의 아들이 안전해서 기쁘다.
I'm glad to be here. 여기 와서 기쁩니다.

Are you prepared? 준비됐나요?
I want to prepare for the test.
나는 그 시험 준비를 하고 싶어요.
Be prepared! 대비하세요!

## Situation 2 What's up?

### 무슨 일이에요?

Julie: Hey Rachel, long time, no see.
안녕, Rachel. 오랜만이야.

Rachel: Hi Julie. Good to see you. What's up?
안녕, Julie. 만나서 반가워, 어떻게 지내?

Julie: Not much. How are you doing?
별일 없어. 어떻게 지내니?

Rachel: Great. Did you do anything special over the vacation?
잘 지내. 방학 동안 뭐 특별한 거라도 했어?

Julie: Just studied for the TOEIC test. How about you?
그냥 토익 공부를 했지. 너는?

Rachel: I went to Thailand for a couple of weeks.
2주 정도 태국에 갔다 왔지.
Have you ever been there?
태국에 가본 적 있니?

Julie: Yeah, just once. I went there last year.
응, 딱 한번 가봤어. 지난해에 갔지.

Rachel: You know, I'm thinking about going abroad next year to study English.
있잖아, 나는 내년에 영어 공부를 하려고 외국에 갈까 생각 중이야.

Julie: Why? There are a lot of places to study here in Korea, for a lot less money.
왜? 한국에도 공부할 곳이 많은데 비용은 훨씬 덜 들고.

Rachel: Language lessons aren't that cheap in Korea. Plus, I've studied English here for years and I still can't speak it well.
한국에서도 어학코스 비용은 그리 싸지 않아. 게다가 내가 한국에서 영어 공부한지 몇 년째인데 아직도 회화를 잘 못해.

Julie: Maybe you're not studying right. A lot of people learn English in Korea.
어쩌면 너의 학습방법이 잘못되었는지도 몰라. 많은 사람들이 한국에서 영어를 공부하거든.

Rachel: Yeah, but most of them only study English or have friends from overseas.
그렇지, 하지만 그들 중 대부분은 영어만 공부하거나 외국 친구를 사귀고 있는 사람들이야.

Julie: True, but you could try to make some new friends.
그렇지, 그런데 너도 노력해서 새로운 친구들을 사귈 수 있잖아.

Rachel: I don't want a friend just to use for English practice. That's rude.
나는 영어연습 할 목적만으로 친구를 사귀고 싶지는 않아. 그건 무례한 행동이야.

Julie: Well, it sounds like you have thought a lot about this. Good luck.
글쎄 이것에 대해 많이 생각했나 보구나. 좋은 결과 있길 바래.

## Upgrade it!

Where are you going on vacation?
휴가 때 어디 갈거니?
Winter vacation is still far away.

겨울 방학은 아직 멀었다.
During the vacation, we are planning to go to Europe.
방학기간 동안에 유럽으로 갈 계획이야.

I want to go abroad.
나는 외국에 가고 싶다.
Studying abroad is a challenge.
외국유학은 도전해 볼만한 일이다.
Have you ever been abroad?
외국에 가 본 적이 있습니까?

You have to learn a lesson.
너는 교훈을 얻어야 한다.
How was the lesson?
수업이 어땠습니까?
How many piano lessons do you have a week?
일주일에 피아노 교습을 몇 번 받습니까?

I want to go overseas.
나는 외국으로 가고 싶다.
Have you ever been overseas?
외국에 가본 적이 있습니까?
We need to research overseas markets.
해외 시장을 조사할 필요가 있습니다.

I tried hard.
나는 열심히 노력하였습니다.
Keep trying!
계속 노력하세요.
Give it a try!
한번 해 보세요.

We need more practice.
우리는 더 연습이 필요합니다.
Practice makes perfect.
연습이 대가를 만듭니다.
You can practice with your partner.
당신의 짝과 연습하세요.

How rude it is!
참 무례하네.
It's not that rude.
그렇게 무례한 것은 아니다.
He said rude things yesterday.
어제 그는 무례한 말을 하였다.

He gave it a lot of thought.
그는 그것에 대해 많이 생각했다.
I thought you needed more time.
네가 더 시간이 필요할 거라고 생각했다.
On second thought, we should do it again.
다시 한 번 생각해보니, 우리는 그것을 다시 한번 해야겠다.

## Unit 02 Caf & Restaurant

### Situation 3 At a Caf

### 카페에서

Cashier1: Hello, welcome to Starbox. How can I help you? 안녕하세요, 스타박스에 잘 오셨습니다. 뭘 도와드릴까요?

Julie: I'll have a large coffee.
커피 큰 걸로 하나 주세요.

Cashier1: Regular or decaf, ma'am?
레귤러로 드릴까요 무카페인으로 드릴까요?

Julie: Decaf, please. How about you, Rachel?
무카페인 주세요. Rachel, 너는 뭘로 할래?

Rachel: I'll have the same. Thanks. 같을 걸로 할게.

Cashier1: Would you like anything else?
뭐 다른 것 필요 없으세요?

Rachel: No, thanks. 없습니다.

Cashier1: That'll be $6.25, please. You can get your drinks over there at the pick-up counter.
6달러 25센트입니다. 저기 픽업 카운터에서 받아가세요.

Cashier2: Two large decafs. Here you go.
무카페인 두 잔 나왔습니다. 여기 있습니다.

Rachel: Thank you. Can you get some cream and sugar for me? 감사합니다. 크림과 설탕 좀 갖다 줄래?

Julie: Sure. 알았어.

Rachel: Have you seen the Herman Hesse exhibition at Busan Museum?
부산 박물관에서 하는 Herman Hesse 전시회 봤어?

Julie: Yes, I went last weekend. It was fantastic. Mike wants to see it, too. You should go together.

응, 지난 주말에 갔었어. 좋았어. Mike도 보고 싶어하는데 너랑 같이 가면 되겠다.

Rachel: Great idea. I'll give him a call later.
좋은 생각이야. 나중에 전화해야겠다.

Julie: Anyway, I sense there is something going on between you two.
어쨌든, 너희들 둘 사이에 뭔가 있는 것 같은 느낌이 들어.

Rachel: What's that supposed to mean? Me and Mike? Oh, no. We are just friends.
무슨 뜻으로 하는 말이야? 나랑 Mike가? 아니야. 우린 그냥 친구 사이야.

Julie: Okay, let's see what happens. People say you guys are going out together a lot recently.
그래, 앞으로 상황을 지켜보지. 사람들이 너희 둘이 최근에 자주 만난다던데.

Rachel: Julie, I'm not going out with him a lot. I mean it. You have my word that there is nothing going on between me and Mike.
Julie, 나는 그와 자주 만나지 않아. 정말이야. Mike와는 정말 별 사이 아니야..

Julie: Alright, alright. Don't get too serious about it.
알았어. 너무 심각하게 받아들이지 마.

Rachel: I just don't want to spoil my friendship with him.
그냥 그와의 우정을 망치고 싶지 않을 뿐이야.

Julie: I understand. Speaking of friendship, aren't you hanging out with Carol lately? I haven't seen you with her recently. Is there anything wrong?
이해해. 우정이라는 이야기가 나왔으니까 말인데 요즘 Carol 만나지 않니? 최근 너랑 같이 있는 걸 못 본 것 같아. 뭐 문제 있는 것은 아니지?

Rachel: Speak of the devil, There is Carol!
호랑이도 제 말하면 온다더니 Carol이 오네.

## Upgrade it!

I usually keep regular hours.
나는 규칙적인 생활을 한다.
I'm in regular work.
나는 정규적인 직업에 종사합니다.
Regular exercise is important for your health.
규칙적인 운동은 건강유지에 중요합니다.

What is the theme of the exhibition?
전시회의 주제가 무엇이니?
I went to the exhibition last month.
지난달 전시회에 갔습니다.
The exhibition was the greatest.
전시회는 최고였다.

It was fantastic.
멋졌다.
That sounds fantastic.
멋진 것 같은데.
This is the most fantastic show I've ever seen.
내가 이제껏 본 것 중 가장 멋진 쇼입니다.
That makes sense.
말이 된다. 수긍이 간다.
Please use a little sense.
상식적으로 생각해 보세요.
I sense much fear in you.
네가 많은 두려움을 느끼고 있다고 느껴진다.

Don't be too serious.
너무 심각하게 생각하지마.
I'm serious.
나는 진지하다. 진담으로 하는 말이다.
There is a serious problem in our robot.
우리의 로봇에 심각한 문제가 있다.

The cookie spoiled my appetite.
쿠키 때문에 입맛을 버렸다.
The rain spoiled my holiday.
비가 와서 휴가가 엉망이 되었다.
The heavy rain spoiled the crops.
폭우가 와서 농사를 망쳤다.

Do you hang out with him?
그랑 어울리니?
Please hang out the flag.
깃발을 거세요.
I don't want to hang out with him anymore.
더 이상 그와 다니지 말아라.

I haven't seen him lately.
최근에 그를 보지 못했다.

He's been working very hard lately.
최근에 그는 매우 열심히 일하고 있다.

What have you been up to lately?
최근에 무슨 일을 하고 있니?
Once a devil, always a devil.
한번 악마는 영원히 악마이다.
She is possessed by a devil.
그녀에게는 악마기 씌었다.

## Situation 4 At a Restaurant

### 식당에서

Host: Good evening. 안녕하세요.
Mike: Mike and Rachel, we have a reservation for 7:00.
Mike와 Rachel인데 일곱 시로 예약했는데요.
Host: Yes. Follow me please. Smoking or non-smoking?
그러세요. 저를 따라오세요. 흡연석 원하세요 비 흡연석 원하세요?
Mike: Non-smoking please.
비 흡연석 부탁합니다.
Host: Will this be alright?
이 자리 마음에 드십니까?
Mike: Do you have a table next to the window?
창가 자리는 없나요?
Host: How is this?
이 자리는 어떻습니까?
Mike: Much better, thank you.
훨씬 좋군요. 감사합니다.
Host: Today's special is rib-eye steak and pasta for $20.
오늘 특별요리는 립아이 스테이크와 파스타인데 20불입니다.
Your waiter will be with you shortly.
담당 웨이터가 곧 올 것입니다.
Rachel: Thank you. Everything looks delicious.
감사합니다. 다 맛있어 보이네.
Waiter: Hello! My name is John. I'll be your waiter this evening.
안녕하십니까? 저의 이름은 John입니다. 오늘 담당 웨이터입니다.
Can I get you anything to drink?
마실 것 좀 갖다 드릴까요?
Mike: I' d like lemonade. 저는 레모네이드 주세요.
Waiter: Sure. And for you, ma'am?
네, 알겠습니다. 여자분은요?
Rachel: I'll have a glass of red wine.
저는 적포도주 한잔 주십시오.
Waiter: Would you like an appetizer?
전채요리 하시겠습니까?
Mike: What do you think, Rachel? Rachel,
어떻게 할래?
Rachel: Let's get this green salad.
여기 그린 샐러드로 하자.
Waiter: Ok, I'll be right back with your drinks and the salad. 알겠습니다.
마실 것과 샐러드를 가지고 금방 오겠습니다.
Mike: It's been a long time since we came here. It's been about a year or so, I guess.
지난 번 여기 오고 시간이 많이 흘렀네. 약 일년 정도 지난 것 같은데.
Rachel: Yeah, that's a long time. We should come here more often.
그래 참 오래되었네. 더 자주 와야겠어.
Mike: I think so, too. Anyhow, we are here to have this great food for ourselves.
나도 그렇게 생각해. 어쨌든, 우리 맛난 것 먹으러 왔잖아.
Rachel: That's right.
그렇지.
Mike: So, how's your school life? Is there any fun?
근데 학교생활은 어때? 재미있니?
Rachel: It's just great. I like what I do there, plus people are friendly.
재미있어. 학교생활도 맘에 들고 사람들도 친절해.
Mike: Good to hear that! 잘됐다.
Waiter: Here are your drinks and salad. Are you ready to order?
여기 음료수와 샐러드 나왔습니다. 주문하실 준비가 되셨습니까?
Rachel: Yes, I'll have the New York steak. 네, 저는 뉴욕 스테이크 하겠습니다.
Waiter: How would you like that?
얼만큼 구워드릴까요?
Rachel: Medium rare, please.
중간 보다 좀 덜 익혀 주세요.
Waiter: Okay. That comes with soup and potato or sweet potato.
알겠습니다. 수프와 감자 혹은 고구마와 함께 나옵니다.
Rachel: I'll have the sweet potato, please.

저는 고구마로 주세요.

Waiter: Thank you, how about you, sir?
감사합니다. 손님은 어떻게 하시겠습니까?

Mike: What's in your seafood spaghetti?
해물 스파게티에는 뭐가 들어가나요?

Waiter: Crab, squid, and clams.
게, 오징어, 대합이 들어갑니다.

Mike: Okay, I'll have that with a cup of onion soup.
그럼 그걸로 주시고 양파수프도 하나 주세요.

Waiter: Will that be all?
그거면 되겠습니까?

Mike: Yes, thank you.
네, 감사합니다.

Waiter: Okay, call me if you need anything else.
다른 게 필요하시면 불러주세요.

### Upgrade it!

I need to make a reservation.
예약을 해야 합니다.
We have serious reservations about the project.
그 프로젝트에 대해서 우리는 심각한 의혹을 품고 있다.
Your reservation for the seminar has been accepted.
당신의 세미나 예약이 접수되었습니다.

You are so special.
당신은 너무나 특별한 사람입니다.
You need special treatment.
당신은 특별한 대우를 받아야 합니다. 당신은 특별한 처치를 받아야 합니다.
Is she someone special to you?
그녀는 네게 특별한 존재니?

It's really delicious.
이것은 정말 맛있다.
I had a delicious lunch with him.
나는 그와 함께 맛있는 점심을 먹었다.
The cookies look really delicious.
이 쿠키는 정말 맛있어 보인다.

Do you want some appetizers?
전채요리를 하시겠습니까?
Enjoy free appetizers!
무료 전채를 즐기세요.
Appetizers will be served in a moment.
전채요리를 곧 내드리겠습니다.

Which salad do you want?
어떤 샐러드를 드시겠습니까?
The fruit salad is on display.
과일 샐러드가 전시되어 있다.
I'd like the chicken salad.
치킨 샐러드로 하겠습니다.

It's sweet.
달다.
How sweet you are!
당신은 참 친절하군요.
I like sweet things.
저는 단 음식을 좋아합니다.

## Unit 03 Movies 영화

### Situation 5 At the movies
### 영화관에서

Rachel: Which movie do you want to see?
어느 영화를 보고 싶니?

Julie: I heard *Ocean's 15* is great.
오션즈 15이 재미있다던데.

Rachel: Hi, two tickets for *Ocean's 15*, please.
오션즈 15으로 두 장 주세요.

Cashier: Ok. For 8 : 00 or 9 : 30?
네, 8시 것 9시 것 중 어느 것으로 하겠습니까?

Rachel: Eight O'clock please. 여덟 시로 주세요.

Cashier: Here are your tickets. That will be $16, please.
여기 표 있습니다. 16불입니다.

Rachel: Here it is.
여기 있습니다.

Cashier: Thank you. Enjoy the movie.
감사합니다. 영화 재미있게 보세요.

Julie: Do you want something to eat?
뭐 좀 먹을래?

Rachel: That's a good idea. How about some popcorn?
좋은 생각이야. 팝콘 어때?

Julie: That would be nice.
좋아.

Rachel: Hi, one large popcorn and two medium

sodas, please.
팝콘 큰거랑 중간 크기 소다 둘 주세요.

Cashier: That'll be $8.
8달러입니다.

Julie: Who is starring in the movie, anyway?
근데 누가 오지?

Rachel: George Clooney, Brad Pitt, Mat Damon, Andy Garcia, and so on, I think.
George Clooney, Brad Pitt, Mat Damon, Andy Garcia 등등이 나와.

Julie: Did you see *Ocean's 14*?
오션즈 14는 봤어?

Rachel: I've seen all the series.
오션즈 시리즈는 다 봤지.

Julie: That's amazing. Which one was the best?
대단하네. 어떤게 젤 재미있데?

Rachel: I think the second one was very exciting.
두 번째 가 재미있더라.

Julie: I think I should rent the DVD. DVD 빌려봐야겠네.

Rachel: That's your call, but you won't regret it.
봐도 후회하지 않을 걸.

## Upgrade it!

I heard that you are new here.
네가 여기 새로 왔다고 들었다.
I've heard a lot about you.
당신에 대해 많이 들었다.

Enjoy your dinner!
저녁 맛있게 드세요.
They are enjoying their meal.
그들은 식사를 맛있게 하고 있다.
We enjoyed listening to the music.
우린 그 음악 듣는 것을 즐겼다.

He became a star.
그는 스타가 되었다.
In the movie he stars as Frodo Baggins.
그 영화에서 그는 Frodo Baggins로 나온다.
It stars Jennifer Aniston.
그 영화에는 Jennifer Aniston이 나온다.

It's really amazing.
정말 멋지다.
It would be an amazing adventure.
멋진 모험이 되겠는걸.
Another amazing fact, you actually came down here to meet me in person.
또 한가지 놀라운 사실은 네가 여기까지 직접 나를 만나러 왔다는 사실이야.

We rented a car yesterday.
우리는 어제 차를 렌트했다.
She rents a house with three other girls.
그녀는 세 명의 여자들과 집을 세로 얻어 같이 쓰고 있다.
She rented rooms to college students.
그녀는 대학생들에게 방들을 세주었다.

I regret having spent the money.
그 돈을 썼던 것을 후회한다.
He regretted his mistake.
그는 그의 실수를 후회하였다.
I have nothing to regret. 나는 후회할 것이 없다.

## Situation 6 What's playing?

### 무슨 영화가 상영됩니까?

Kevin: Do you want to see a movie tonight?
오늘 밤 영화보고 싶니?

Carol: Hmm. Maybe. What's playing?
음 그럴까, 무슨 영화가 있는데?

Kevin: How about the new James Bond film? I heard it's really exciting.
새로 나온 James Bond 영화는 어때? 정말 재미있다더라.

Carol: Actually, the last one was rather boring.
사실 지난 번 것은 좀 지루했어.

Kevin: What about the movie based on Stephen King's new novel?
Stephen King의 신작소설을 영화화한 것은 어때?

Carol: I don't know. His books are usually fascinating, but I don't like horror movies.
잘 모르겠네. 그의 작품들은 주로 재미있지만 난 공포영화는 좋아하지 않아.

Kevin: Well, what do you want to see?
글쎄, 뭘 보고 싶니?

Carol: I'm interested in the new Halle Berry movie. It looks good.

Halle Berry의 새로운 영화가 보고 싶어. 괜찮을 것 같은데.

Kevin: Hmm. I personally don't like Halle Berry, but if you insist.
음. 나는 개인적으로 Halle Berry를 좋아하지 않아. 하지만 네가 굳이 보겠다면

Carol: You don't have to. How about the new Japanese animation?
꼭 그럴 필요는 없어. 새로 나온 일본 애니메이션은 어떨까?

Kevin: You mean The Girl Who Leapt Through Time? '시간을 달리는 소녀' 말하는 거니?

Carol: Yes, I heard that movie is well-made and it makes us think.
응, 그 영화가 잘 만들어졌고 생각하게끔 한다던데.

Kevin: I don't know what to say. I don't particularly like Japanese movies.
뭐라 해야 할지 모르겠네. 난 일본영화는 특히 안 좋아해서.

Carol: I think we have a problem here. That means you really want to see the James Bond film, and there is no alternative.
이거 문제네. 너는 James Bond 영화를 꼭 봐야 하겠고 다른 것은 안 된다는 거잖아.

Kevin: I'm afraid so. Carol. Please. I really want to see the movie, and all my other friends have already seen the movie. I don't want to watch it alone.
그렇네. Carol, 부탁이야. 나는 그 영화를 꼭 보고 싶어. 그리고 다른 내 친구들은 그 영화를 다 봤단 말이야. 혼자 보기는 싫어.

Carol: Alright, alright, alright. That's enough. Don't grumble about it. 알았어 그만해, 칭얼거리지 마. Let's see what you want to see today, and next time we watch what I want. Deal?
오늘은 네가 보고 싶은 걸 보고 다음 번엔 내가 보고 싶은 것 본다. 오케이?

Kevin: Deal! Thanks Carol. You are always so generous and forgiving. I'm so lucky to have a friend like you. 오케이! 고마워 Carol. 넌 항상 맘이 넓고 관용이 넘친다니까. 너와 같은 친구를 두어서 난 정말 운이 좋아.

Carol: Don't flatter me! Let's go. 아부 그만하고 가자.

## Upgrade it!

I would rather die than yield.
항복하느니 차라리 죽겠다.
I feel rather better today.

난 기분이 다소 좋아졌어.
I would die rather than yield.
항복할 바에 죽음을 택하겠다.

It's so fascinating.
정말 멋지다.
She is a fascinating speaker.
그녀는 멋진 연설가이다.
It's a fascinating city.
이곳은 멋진 도시이다.

There are several well-made movies recently.
최근 잘 만들어진 영화가 몇 편 있습니다.
The books are well-made.
이 책은 잘 쓰여진 것입니다.
It's well-made.
그것은 잘 만들어졌다.

I don't particularly like the movie.
나는 특히 그 영화를 좋아하지 않는다.
That necklace looks particularly attractive on you.
그 목걸이는 네가 하니까 특히 어울린다.
The homework is particularly important.
그 숙제는 특히 중요하다.

No alternative is left.
다른 대안이 없다.
What alternative do we have?
우리는 어떤 대안이 있지?

He grumbles about everything.
그는 모든 것에 대해 불평한다.
She grumbled over the food.
그녀는 음식에 대해서 불평하였다.
He grumbles at his father all the time.
그는 항상 그의 아버지에 대해 불평한다.
He is so generous.
그는 대단히 관대하다.
You are a generous giver.
너는 관대하게 베푸는 사람이다.

He is forgiving.
그는 용서를 잘 한다.
How forgiving are you?
당신은 정말 관용적인 사람입니다.
I'm not very forgiving.
난 그다지 관용적인 사람이 아니다.

## Unit 04 Dating 데이트하기

### Situation 7 Set me up!

**소개시켜줘!**

Julie: I'd like to have a boyfriend.
남자친구를 사귀고 싶어.

Rachel: I can set you up with my best friend. He's interested in meeting someone, too.
나랑 가장 친한 친구를 소개시켜 줄 수 있어. 걔도 누군가를 만나고 싶어해.

Julie: What does he look like? 어떻게 생겼니?

Rachel: He's kind of tall and very good-looking. He has dark hair and a great smile.
키가 좀 크고 매우 잘 생겼어. 머리는 검고 미소가 멋지지.

Julie: What's he like? 성격은?

Rachel: He's charming and has a great sense of humor, but he can be a little stubborn from time to time.
매력적이고 유머감각이 뛰어나. 하지만 가끔씩 고집 피울 때도 있어.

Julie: Sounds like I should give it a try.
한번 만나봐야 할 것 같은데.

Rachel: Of course you should. He's a great guy. Let's say this Saturday. Is it alright?
당연하지. 그는 멋진 남자야. 이번 토요일로 하지 어때?

Julie: Let me check my schedule. Oh, my parents are coming this weekend. I have to be with them all weekend.
내 스케줄을 확인해 볼게. 아 우리 부모님께서 이번 주말에 오시네. 주말 내내 부모님과 함께 있어야만 해.

Rachel: Oh, then how about next Wednesday after school?
그래 그럼 다음 주 수요일 학교 마치고는 어때?

Julie: That sounds fine with me. 괜찮아.

Rachel: Alright. Then, I will tell him all the good things about you, and convince him that he should meet you.
좋았어. 그럼 걔한테 너에 대한 좋은 말을 많이 해 줘서 널 꼭 만나보고 싶은 맘이 들도록 할게.

Julie: Thanks, but don't brag about me too much.
고마워 하지만 너무 과장된 말은 하지마.

Rachel: No worries.
걱정하지마.

### Upgrade it!

Are you interested in him?
당신은 그에게 관심이 있습니까?
If you are interested, please give us a call.
관심 있으면 우리에게 전화주세요.
We invited all the people who were interested.
우리는 관심있는 사람을 다 초대했다.
I met a guy who was very charming.
대단히 매력적인 남자를 만났다.
She is charming. 그녀는 매혹적이다.
It's not easy to find a Prince Charming.
백마 탄 왕자님을 만나는 것은 쉽지 않다.

He has no common sense.
그는 상식이 없다.
It makes plenty of sense.
대단히 지당하다.
It makes no sense.
그건 말도 안 된다.

He is as stubborn as a mule.
그는 대단히 고집스럽다.
In general, they are stubborn rather than cooperative.
일반적으로 그들은 협조적이라기보다는 고집스럽다.
You are just being stubborn.
넌 고집을 피우고 있다.

It's not easy to convince him.
그를 설득하는 것은 쉽지 않다.
We convinced her of her error.
우리는 그녀에게 그녀가 실수했다는 것을 확신시켰다.
I can convince him.

내가 그를 설득할 수 있다.

He always brags about his rich father.
그는 항상 그의 부자 아빠에 대해 자랑한다.
It's just nothing to brag about.
뭐 별 자랑할 만할 일도 아니에요.
Don't brag!
허풍피지 마라.

## Situation 8 How did Your Date Go?

### 데이트 잘 되었니?

Rachel: Tell me about your date last night.
어젯밤 데이트 얘기 좀 해봐라.

Julie: It was good at first. We were having a nice meal at a fine restaurant, when he suddenly realized he forgot to bring his wallet.
처음에는 좋았어. 멋진 식당에서 맛있는 음식을 먹고 있는데 갑자기 그가 지갑을 두고 온 것을 깨달은 거야.

Rachel: Oh, no! What did you do?
저런 세상에. 그래서 어떻게 했어?

Julie: He tried to get his roommate to bring his wallet to the restaurant, but his roomie was studying at the library.
그가 자기 룸메이트를 시켜서 지갑을 식당에 가져오도록 하려고 했는데 룸메이트가 도서관에서 공부하고 있었던 거야.

Rachel: What happened then? 그래서?

Julie: I had to wait for about 30 minutes while he went back home to get his wallet.
그가 자기 집에 돌아가 지갑을 가져오는 동안 나는 30분 정도 기다려야 했지.

Rachel: How embarrassing! Didn't you have any money, anyway?
저런 난처한 일이. 넌 돈이 없었니?

Julie: I did, but he insisted that he should pay.
있었지. 근데 그가 굳이 자기가 내겠다고 우기는 거야.

Rachel: That's ridiculous. 말도 안 된다.

Julie: Anyway, after the dinner, we kind of had some quality time together.
어쨌든 그렇게 저녁 식사를 하고 난 후에 함께 좋은 시간을 보냈어.

Rachel: What's that supposed to mean? After THAT dinner, you guys went to other places and had fun? I don't get it.
그게 무슨 말이야? 저녁식사 사건 후 다른 데로 가서 좋은 시간을 가졌다고. 난 이해가 안 되는데.

Julie: Other than the dinner incident, he was very nice, kind, and even very funny.
저녁식사 사건 말고는 아주 괜찮고 친절하고 재미있기까지 하던걸.

Rachel: Good to hear that. 잘됐다.

Julie: Thanks Rachel! You are my best friend.
고마워 Rachel. 넌 나의 가장 친한 친구야.

Rachel: I hope you guys get along well.
너희들이 잘 되었으면 좋겠어.

## Upgrade it!

Fine feathers make fine birds.
좋은 깃털이 좋은 새를 만든다.
That's fine with me.
나는 괜찮아.

She cried out suddenly.
그녀는 갑자기 울었다.
He was suddenly taken ill.
그는 갑자기 병들었다.
The car stopped suddenly.
차가 갑자기 멈춰 섰다.

I was in an embarrassing situation.
나는 황당한 상황에 처했다.
That's very embarrassing.
대단히 당황스럽다.
It's embarrassing to talk about myself.
내 자신에 대해 이야기 하는 것은 쑥스러운 일이다.

He continued to insist that I misled him.
내가 잘못된 정보를 주었다고 그는 계속 주장하였다.
She insisted that the pen was hers.
그녀는 그 펜이 자기 것이라고 우겼다.
If you insist on smoking in the restaurant, you will be asked to leave.
계속 식당 안에서 담배를 피우시겠다면 나가 주세요.
You are making a ridiculous claim.
너는 말도 안 되는 주장을 하고 있다.

I've never heard anything so ridiculous.
나는 이제껏 그렇게 웃기는 말을 들어본 적이 없다.
You look ridiculous.
너 참 이상해 보인다.

He bought some quality furniture.
그는 고급 가구를 샀다.
They are the best quality you can buy.
당신이 살 수 있는 최상의 품질 입니다.
I need some quality time.
나는 좋은 시간을 보냈다.

## Unit 05 Feeling 감정

### Situation 9 I need to be refreshed.

### 재 충전이 필요해

Mark: Hey, what's up?
왜 그래 무슨 일 있니?
Julie: I'm really depressed these days. I don't know why.
요즘 너무 우울해. 왠지 모르겠어.
Mark: Is that because you broke up with your boyfriend?
남자친구랑 헤어져서 그래?
Julie: No, it's not that. I just think I am missing something important in my life.
아니야 그게 아냐. 그냥 인생에 중요한 뭔가를 놓치고 있다는 느낌이 들어서.
Mark: You see? I said you need a new boyfriend.
거봐. 새로운 남자친구가 필요하다고 했지?
Julie: Hello, I said I am so over him!
이봐 정말 그를 깨끗이 잊었다니까.
I don't have any feelings for him at all.
아무런 감정도 남아 있지 않아.
Mark: Well, if you ask me, I can say this.
글쎄 이런 말을 해주고 싶네.
Look at those couples. They look so happy together. When they are together, I'm sure they feel they have everything.
저기 커플을 봐. 같이 참 행복해 보이지. 함께 있으면 세상을 다 가진 것처럼 느낄 거야.
Julie: I think she chose him because he's rich, if you ask me.
내 생각에는 그녀가 그를 선택한 것은 그의 재력 때문인 것 같은데.
He certainly isn't attractive to me.
확실한 것은 그는 나에겐 매력적이지 않다는 거지.
Mark: Hmm··· Julie, what's got into you? You really need something to make you refreshed.
Julie
너 갑자기 왜 그러니? 정말 넌 뭔가 재충전이 필요한 것 같아.
Julie: The point is I need something to improve my life. And I want to learn some different things.
중요한 것은 나의 인생을 향상시켜 줄 뭔가가 필요하다는 것이지. 뭔가 다른 것들을 배우고 싶어.
Mark: And you know where I am, if you need me.
네가 도움이 필요할 때는 언제나 내가 도와줄게.
Julie: Thanks. I'm thinking of taking a trip to Canada for a while to meet my old friends. It will be great. I hope to spend time thinking of ways to better my life.
고마워. 당분간 옛 친구들을 만나러 캐나다로 여행이라도 갈 생각이야. 좋은 시간이 될 거야. 내 삶을 좀 더 윤택하게 할 방법들에 대해 생각해보고 싶어.
Mark: What can I say?
I guess you are just special. I cannot wait to see you with the better life you want.
뭐라고 해야 할까? 내 생각에 넌 참 특별한 것 같아. 네가 원하는 향상된 삶을 사는 너의 모습을 빨리 보고 싶어.
Julie: Well, we should go back into the class again, and thank you. I feel much better now.
근데 우리 다시 수업에 들어가야 하잖아. 고마워. 기분이 한결 좋아졌어.
Mark: Don't mention it. I want to say thank YOU for having a chance to talk to you.
천만에 내가 오히려 고맙지 너랑 얘기할 수 있어서.

### Upgrade it!

He's improved a lot!
그는 많이 향상되었다.
I'm gonna improve my English.
저는 영어실력을 향상시킬 것입니다.

I feel depressed.
나는 우울하다.
Don't make yourself depressed.

우울해하지 마세요.

This is a very important subject to study.
이것은 중요한 공부과목이다.
Do something important.
뭔가 중요한 것을 하십시오.

I don't wanna break the rule.
나는 규칙을 위반하고 싶지 않다.
Let's take a break.
휴식을 합시다.
They just broke up.
그들은 막 헤어졌다.

I need something to refresh myself.
뭔가 기분전환이 필요하다.
She felt refreshed.
그녀는 상쾌함을 느꼈다.
There are some refreshments in the room.
방에 음료수가 있습니다.

She is very precious to me.
그녀는 내게 소중한 존재이다.
She is crazy about precious stones.
그녀는 보석을 매우 좋아한다.
I can say she is a very precious friend.
그녀는 매우 소중한 친구이다.

Do you want something special?
뭔가 특별한 것을 원하십니까?
This is very special.
이것은 아주 특별하다.
I don't want to read TV specials.
TV특집을 읽기 싫다.

Don't mention it.
천만에요. 별 말씀을..
Do you have anything to mention to me?
내게 말할 것이 있으세요?

Chances are, he's gonna survive.
아마 그는 살아남을 것이다.
I got a chance.
나는 기회가 있었다.
Fifty percent chance of shower today!
오늘 비가 올 확률은 50%이다.

Thank you for giving me a chance.
제게 기회를 주셔서 감사합니다.

## Situation 10 You look more human.
## 당신은 더 인간적으로 보입니다.

Julie: Are you okay? You look tired.
괜찮니? 피곤해 보이는데.
Jeff: I'm feeling under the weather.
컨디션이 좋지 않아.
Julie: Why don't you take a break?
좀 쉬지 그래?
Jeff: I can't. I have to finish this today.
그럴 수 없어. 이것을 오늘 마쳐야 하거든.
Julie: You know you should take care of your health when you're still young.
젊은 시절에 건강을 돌보아야 해.
Do you want some chocolate cookies and some tea?
초콜릿 쿠키와 차 좀 줄까?
Jeff: No. I lost my appetite. 아니 식욕을 잃었어.
Well, I'll just have a cup of tea then.
그냥 차나 한잔 마실래.
Julie: Okay, here you are. Be careful. It's very hot.
좋아 여기 있어. 조심해, 매우 뜨거우니까.
Jeff: Thanks. I feel much better now.
고마워. 훨씬 나아졌어.
Julie: You know, you're impressing everyone. But you work too much.
넌 모든 사람의 인정을 받고 있어. 하지만 너무 일을 많이 하는 것 같아.
Jeff: Do you think it's a problem?
그게 무슨 문제라도 되니?
Julie: No, but all work and no play makes you feel stressed.
아니 그냥 일만하고 쉬지 않으면 스트레스를 받으니까.
Jeff: You're right.
네 말이 맞아.
Julie: By the way, what's that thing on your shirt?
근데 셔츠에 뭐가 묻었어?
Jeff: What? Gee… it's coffee! I had coffee this morning.
뭐? 에이 커피가 묻었네. 오늘 아침 커피를 마셨어.
This is my favorite shirt.
내가 좋아하는 셔츠인데.
Julie: Don't worry. I'm sure we can get it off.

걱정 마, 꼭 얼룩을 빼낼 수 있을 거야.

Jeff: I'm not myself today. You think I am terrible today, right?
오늘 내가 왜 이러지. 네가 봐도 내가 오늘 엉망이지, 그지?

Julie: No, it's not that. What can I say? You look more human.
아니. 뭐랄까 좀더 인간적으로 보여.

## Upgrade it!

You're impressing everyone.
당신은 모든 사람들에게 인정을 받고 있다.
He is very impressive.
그는 매우 인상적이다.
She's always trying to impress others.
그녀는 항상 다른 사람들에게 인상을 깊게 남기려고 노력한다.

I have to finish this today.
저는 오늘 이것을 끝내야 합니다.
Just finish your meal.
빨리 식사를 마치세요.
Can you see the finish line there?
저기 있는 결승선이 보이세요?

Keep your health while you're still young.
아직 젊을 때 건강은 지키세요.
I go to the health club every evening.
저는 매일 저녁 헬스클럽에 갑니다.
He has some health problems.
그는 건강상의 문제가 좀 있습니다.
This is the health care centre.
이곳은 의료시설입니다.

She has a big appetite.
그녀는 왕성한 식욕을 가지고 있습니다.
I lost my appetite.
나는 식욕을 잃었다.
Be careful!
조심하세요.
She is a careful driver.
그녀는 운전을 조심스럽게 한다.
You need to be careful.
너는 조심할 필요가 있다.

No problem.
문제 없어요.
She has a big problem.
그녀는 큰 곤란에 빠졌다.
What's your problem?
너의 문제가 무엇이니?

This is my favorite subject.
이것은 내가 좋아하는 과목이다.
What's your favorite food?
네가 좋아하는 음식이 무엇이지?
My favorite color is blue.
내가 좋아하는 색은 푸른색이다.

Oh, no! I'm not myself today!
이런 내가 오늘 왜 이러지?
Look at yourself in the mirror.
거울에 비친 네 모습을 보아라.
I'll do it myself. 제가 하겠습니다.

# Unit 06 Airport 공항

## Situation 11 This airport is crowded.
## 이 공항은 붐빈다.

Julie: This airport is always crowded!
이 공항은 항상 붐빈다.

Ann: Look out and keep all your bags close to you. They can easily be stolen.
조심해 그리고 가방을 몸에 붙이고 다녀. 도난의 우려가 있거든.

Julie: Yeah, you can say that again.
그래 그렇지.

Ann: You know, causing problems at the airport is just horrible to think about, especially when you are on a vacation.
공항에서 문제가 생기는 것은 생각만 해도 끔직해 특히 휴가여행을 떠날 때는.

Julie: I know, and where's the check in counter?
그럼 근데 체크인 카운터는 어디지?
We should get our boarding passes.
탑승권을 받아야 하는데.

Ann: It's right over there. 바로 저기에 있어.
Isn't it better to wait for Mark?

Mark를 기다리는 것이 좋지 않을까?

Julie: He said he would be at the airport sometime soon. I just got his message.
곧 공항에 도착한다고 그가 말했는데. 방금 연락이 왔어.

Ann: Then, let's go to the counter first and be ready for ticketing.
그럼 우선 카운터로 가서 발권 준비를 하자.

Julie: We can wait for him there.
거기서 그를 기다리면 되겠다.

Ann: Is it the direct flight to Vancouver?
밴쿠버 직항 편이니?

Julie: No. We're gonna stop in Tokyo and transfer to the connecting flight to Vancouver there.
아니 도쿄를 경유해서 밴쿠버 연결편을 탈 거야.

Ann: Wow, I can hang around Tokyo while waiting then.
와! 그럼 기다리는 동안에 도쿄 구경을 할 수 있겠다.

Julie: Well, we are not allowed to leave the airport. Or else, we must pay the tax again.
글쎄 공항 밖으로 나갈 수 없는데. 나가려면 세금을 다시 내야 해.

Ann: Hmm... That's troublesome. 음 그건 곤란한데.
By the way, you just have two bags?
근데 가방이 두 개뿐이니?

Julie: Yes, this suitcase, and I'll carry this small bag on with me.
응, 이 옷 가방이랑 이 작은 가방을 가지고 탈 거야.
Do you have three bags to check in?
너는 부칠 가방이 세 개야?

Ann: No, these two. I'll carry this one with me.
I hope it is not overweight.
아니 이것 두 개야. 이 가방은 가지고 탈 거야. 중량초과가 안돼야 할 텐데.

Julie: I don't think so. 괜찮을 것 같은데.
Oh, here he comes at last! Hey, Mark, over here!
어 저기 Mark가 드디어 온다. Mark 여기야!

## Upgrade it!

The city street is always crowded.
이 도시의 거리는 항상 붐빈다.
Look at the crowd!
저 군중을 보라!
They are close friends.
그들은 가까운 친구입니다.
The airport is close to your house.
그 공항은 우리 집에서 가깝다.
Come close to me.
내게 가까이 오너라.

They are boarding the plane.
그들이 비행기에 탑승하고 있다.
Show me your boarding pass.
저에게 탑승권을 보여주세요.
They are on board.
그들은 탑승하고 있다.

I'm still healthy.
그는 여전히 건강하다.
Are you still at work?
당신은 아직도 그 일을 하십니까?

He's right.
그가 옳아.
Turn right at the end of the street.
길 끝에서 우회전 하세요.
You spelled your name right.
당신은 당신의 이름의 철자를 올바로 썼습니다.

Where's the check-in counter?
체크인 카운터가 어디입니까?
Please cash this check.
이 수표를 현금으로 바꿔주세요.
What do you want to check?
뭘 확인하고 싶으세요?

He transferred to another branch.
그는 다른 부서로 옮겨갔다.
I will transfer to the connecting flight.
저는 연결편으로 갈아탑니다.
I will transfer to bus number 50.
저는 50번 버스로 갈아탑니다.

I'll connect you to this department.
이 부서로 전화를 연결해 드리겠습니다.
This is the connecting flight.
이것은 연결편입니다.
Please connect me to the Personnel Department.
인사과로 전화를 연결해 주세요.

## Situation 12 In-flight

### 기내 안에서

Ann: Flight AA 701 to Vancouver Seat 24L .
Well, this is my first time to take an international flight.
It's thrilling!
밴쿠버 행 AA 701편 24L좌석이라. 처음으로 국제선을 타는 거라 흥분되네.

Mark: It's almost the same as a domestic flight, but the in-flight meal is somewhat different on the menu.
국내선이랑 거의 비슷해. 하지만 기내식이 메뉴가 좀 달라.
Oh, I'm hungry.
아 배고프다.

Ann: I'm hungry, too. When do they serve lunch?
나도 배가 고프다. 점심은 언제 주지?

Mark: Mm… I can smell chicken.
음 닭고기 냄새가 나는데..
Oh, my stomach is rumbling now.
이제는 위장에서 천둥소리가 나네.

Flight Attendant: Hello.
안녕하세요.

Mark: Hi.
안녕하세요.

Flight Attendant: Chicken, salmon, or vegetarian?
치킨, 연어, 채식 식단 중 어느 것을 원하십니까?

Mark: Chicken, please.
치킨으로 주세요.

Flight Attendant: Anything to drink?
마실 것 하시겠습니까?

Mark: Yes, some red wine, please.
네, 적포도주 주세요.

Flight Attendant: Here you are.
여기 있습니다.

Mark: Thank you.
감사합니다.

Flight Attendant: And for you, ma'am? Chicken, salmon, or vegetarian?
그리고 여자손님은요? 치킨, 연어, 채식식단 중 고르실 수 있습니다.

Ann: Salmon, please.
연어 주세요.

Flight Attendant: And any drink?
마실 건요?

Ann: Yes, just water, please.
네, 그냥 물 주세요.

Flight Attendant: With or without gas?
가스가 있는 걸로 드릴까요? 없는 걸로 드릴까요?

Ann: Sorry? I don't understand.
뭐라고요? 이해를 못하겠는데.

Flight Attendant: This is Evian without gas. And this is Perrier with gas.
이건 가스가 없는 에비앙이고 이것은 가스가 있는 페리어입니다.

Ann: Oh, yes. Evian, please.
아, 네. 에비앙으로 주세요.

Flight Attendant: Here you are. Enjoy your meal.
여기 있습니다. 맛있게 드세요.

Ann: Thank you. Wow, it looks delicious!
감사합니다. 와 맛있겠다.

Mark: Yes, I'm really enjoying it. 그럼 정말 맛있네.
Oh, and don't forget to fill in your immigration card after your meal.
밥 먹고 입국신고서 작성하는 것 잊지마.

Ann: What's that? 그게 뭔데?

Mark: They check your immigration card and your passport when you arrive, and ask a few questions.
네가 도착하면 그들이 너의 입국신고서와 여권을 검사할 거야.

Ann: Like what?
어떤 걸 쓰는 거지?

Mark: Like… the purpose of your visit or the place you are staying, and so on.
방문의 목적이나 묵을 곳 등등이지.

Ann: All right. Uh, do you have a pen? 알았어. 펜 있어?

Mark: No, I don't, sorry. Julie may have one, I guess.
아니 Julie가 있을 걸.
She's always well prepared.
항상 준비를 잘 하니까.

### Upgrade it!

This is the connecting flight.
이것은 연결편입니다.
Flight AA 701 to Vancouver.
밴쿠버 행 AA701편.

This is the last flight.
이것은 마지막 비행기입니다.

They are different.
그들은 다르다.
This room is different from yours.
이 방은 너의 방과 다르다.
What's the difference?
차이가 무엇입니까?
It makes no difference.
차이가 없습니다.

They are going to attend the international conference.
그들은 국제회의에 참석할 것입니다.
This is the international airport.
이것은 국제공항입니다.
I take the international flight.
저는 국제선을 탑니다.

Just give me anything.
제게 무엇이라도 주세요.
Anything to drink?
마실 것 하시겠습니까?
I don't like to do anything.
나는 무엇도 하고 싶지 않다.

I cannot live without you.
나는 너 없이 살 수 없다.
I want some water without gas.
저는 가스가 없는 물을 원합니다.
Without your help, I would not succeed.
당신의 도움이 없이 성공하지 못할 것입니다.

I really enjoyed the show.
그 쇼를 정말 재미있게 보았습니다.
Enjoy yourself.
재미있는 시간 가지세요.

I want to be prepared.
나는 준비를 갖추고 싶다.
All things are prepared.
다 준비되었다.
He is preparing something.
그는 무엇인가를 준비하고 있다.

## Unit 07 Travel 여행

### Situation 13 There are many attractions in this

**이 도시에는 가볼 곳이 많이 있습니다.**

Julie: I just want to look around before dinner.
저녁식사 전 구경 좀 하고 싶다.
Do you want to join me? 같이 갈래?

Ann: Sure, but what about Mike?
좋아 근데 Mike는 어쩌지?

Julie: He stepped out to exchange some money.
그는 환전하러 밖으로 나갔어.
I think he's just hanging around alone somewhere.
어딘가 혼자서 구경하고 있을 것 같은데.
So, are you ready to go?
갈 준비 되었니?

Ann: Yes. Where is the best place to look around?
I want to see a museum or park.
응, 구경하기 가장 좋은 곳이 어디지? 박물관이나 공원을 보고 싶은데.

Julie: Let's drop by the Visitor's Center first.
관광객센터에 들러보자.
We can get some information and some city maps there.
정보를 얻을 수 있을 거고 도시 지도도 구할 수 있을 거야.

Ann: Okay, that's good. 좋았어. 그거 좋겠어.

Julie: I saw one right across the street. Oh, there it is.
길 건너자마자 하나 있던데. 어 저기에 있네.

Ann: You've been here in Vancouver, right?
너 이전에 밴쿠버에 와 봤구나. 그렇지?

Julie: Yes, but it was long ago.
응 하지만 오래 전이었어.

Ann: Here we are. 도착했어.
Excuse me. Can I get a map of this city?
실례합니다. 도시 지도 한 장 구할 수 있을까요?

Clerk: Sure. Here it is.
그럼요 여기 있습니다.

Ann: Thanks. We have almost a month in this city. What places are good to look around?
감사합니다. 이 도시에 거의 한달 정도 머물러야 합니다. 구경할 만한 곳이 어디입니까?

Clerk: Well, there are beautiful parks along the beach and you can also enjoy the markets or concerts.

글쎄요, 해변가로 멋진 공원이 몇 개 있고 시장과 콘서트도 구경할 수 있겠네요.
You can find all the places on the map.
이 지도상에 다 나옵니다.

Ann: Thanks. Where's the nearest market around here?
감사합니다. 이 주변에서 가장 가까운 시장에 어디입니까?

Clerk: You can see it on the map here.
여기 지도상에 있네요.
There's one right past the theater.
극장 지나자마자 하나 있습니다.

## Upgrade it!

Will you join us?
우리랑 같이 가시겠습니까?
I'd like to join the tour.
저는 투어에 같이 가고 싶습니다.

I just want to hang around.
그냥 구경 좀 하고 싶어요.
Please hang it on the wall.
이것을 벽에 걸어 주세요.
Don't hang up the phone.
제발 전화를 끊지 말아 주세요.
The murderer was hanged last year.
그 살인자는 지난해 교수형을 당했다.

This is my place.
이곳이 우리 집입니다.
Where is the best place to look around?
구경하기 좋은 곳이 어디입니까?
I like that place there.
저는 저기 있는 장소가 좋습니다.

He just stepped out.
그는 방금 나갔다.
Watch your step!
발 밑을 조심하세요.
Just a few steps will take you to that place.
몇 발자국만 더 가면 그 장소에 도착할 것이다.
They went about the work step by step.
그 일을 단계적으로 진행했다.

I need some information
저는 정보가 좀 필요합니다.
Where is the Information Centre?
정보센터가 어디입니까?
If you search the web, you can get a lot of information.
인터넷 검색을 해보면 많은 정보를 얻을 수 있다.

I have several questions to ask.
몇 가지 질문할 것이 있습니다.
There are several beautiful parks.
아름다운 공원이 몇 개 있습니다.
Several people are standing out there.
몇몇 사람들이 밖에 서 있다.

The Stock Market has crashed.
주식시장이 붕괴되었다.
I've got some stuff to buy at the market.
시장에서 살 물건이 좀 있다.
This is the marketplace.
이곳은 시장입니다.

## Situation 14 I'd like to reserve tickets.
## 표를 예매하고 싶습니다.

Mark: I was trying to get some information but the Internet was too slow.
정보를 구하려고 했는데 인터넷이 너무 느렸어요.
I couldn't reserve tickets through the Internet.
인터넷상으로 예매를 못했어요.

Julie: That's okay. I'd rather buy tickets in person. 괜찮아요. 직접 표를 구매하는 것도 재미있어요.
It is much more romantic. Do you have the Theater Guide book?
그것이 더 낭만적이거든요. 극장 안내책자 있어요?

Mark: No, but I can see one here on this shelf.
아니요. 하지만 여기 선반에 하나 있네요.

Julie: Let me check the schedule. 일정을 확인합시다.
How many shows do they have tonight?
오늘 몇 차례 상영하나요?

Mark: Well, there are shows at 7:00 and 9:00.
7시와 9시에 상영하네요.
I'm not sure if we can get tickets for tonight.
오늘밤 표를 구할 수 있을는지 모르겠어요.
Why don't we reserve tickets for this Saturday?
토요일 표를 예약하는 게 어때요?

Julie: You know I'm going on a camping trip to the Jasper area with my friends this Saturday.
이번 주 토요일에는 친구들이랑 제스퍼 지역으로 캠핑하는데요.

Mark: Oh, is it this weekend? 그게 이번 주말이었나?

Julie: Yes. If you want, you and Ann can also join us.
네. 당신의 원하시면 앤과 함께 와도 좋아요.

Mark: I'd love to.
좋아요.

Julie: Now, it's our turn. I think the 7:00 o'clock show will be better.
이제 우리 차례입니다. 일곱 시 것이 더 좋을 것 같아요.

Mark: Okay. Hi, do you have tickets for the 7:00 o'clock show tonight?
좋아요. 안녕하세요. 오늘 일곱 시 표가 있나요?

Clerk: Yes. We still have a few seats left. How many, sir?
네, 아직 몇 장 남아 있습니다. 몇 장이나 드릴까요?

Mark: Just two, please. I'll pay by cash.
두 장만 주세요. 현금으로 계산하겠습니다.

Clerk: All right. That's $36.
좋습니다. 36달러입니다.

Mark: There you go. Oh, one more thing.
여기 있습니다. 아 한가지만 더요.
Are there any good tourist sites near here?
이 근처에 구경할 만한 관광지가 있습니까?
We still have 3 more hours.
아직 세시간이나 남았거든요.

Clerk: How about Starry Park? 스타리 공원은 어때요?
You can take a walk and enjoy shopping for some souvenirs on the way.
산책도 할 수 있고 도중에 기념품도 살 수 있어요.

Mark: Oh. That's a good idea. Thanks a lot.
좋은 생각이에요. 감사합니다.

Clerk: You're welcome. 천만에요.

## Upgrade it!

The table is reserved.
이 테이블은 예약석입니다.
I'd like to reserve a seat.
자리를 예약하고 싶다.
Have you reserved a table for dinner?
저녁식사 예약을 했나요?

I can't get through.
통화연결이 안 된다.
This tunnel goes through the city.
이 터널은 도시를 관통한다.
You should look through the file.
당신은 파일을 조사해 봐야 한다.

I got a speeding ticket.
속도위반 딱지를 받았다.
Do you have tickets for the show?
공연 표가 있습니까?
Tickets, please. 표 주세요.

He just showed up.
그는 방금 나타났다.
I want to enjoy tonight's show.
저는 오늘 밤 공연을 즐기고 싶습니다.
What time is the first show?
첫 공연이 몇 시입니까?
Just show it to me.
그것을 제게 보여주세요.

Will you cash this for me?
이것을 현금으로 바꾸어 주시겠어요?
Cash or credit card?
현금으로 하시겠어요 카드로 하시겠어요?
I'll pay by cash.
현금으로 내겠습니다.

This way, please.
이 쪽으로 오세요.
Is this the right way to go?
이 길이 맞습니까?
This is the way he made a lot of money.
이런 방법으로 그는 많은 돈을 벌었다.

This is the souvenir shop.
이것은 기념품 가게입니다.
I want some souvenirs for my son.
제 아들에게 줄 기념품을 사고 싶습니다.
It can be a souvenir.
그건 기념품이 될 수 있겠다.

## Unit 08 Direction 방향

### Situation 15 Turn right at the end of the 길 끝에서 우회전 하세요.

Mark: Will you take a walk to Starry Park?
스타리 공원으로 산책갈래?
Julie: Starry Park? Okay. That's good.
스타리 공원? 좋았어.
Mark: We can enjoy bike riding and the beautiful beach there.
자전거도 탈 수 있고 멋진 해변도 볼 수 있어.
Julie: That's a good idea. 좋은 생각이야.
Mark: We can have dinner at the nearby restaurant after that.
그리고 나서 근처 식당에서 저녁을 먹을 수 있어.
Julie: Yeah. Do you know which way we should go to the park?
좋아. 어디로 가야 공원으로 가는지 아니?
Mark: Let me ask.
내가 물어볼게.
Excuse me. How can I get to Starry Park from here?
실례합니다. 여기서 스타리 공원으로 가려면 어떻게 해야 하나요?
Man: Well, it's not far. You can walk that way.
여기서 멀지 않아요. 저쪽으로 걸어가시면 되요.
Just go straight. 곧장 쭉 가세요.
Mark: Thank you so much.
대단히 감사합니다.
Man: No trouble.
천만에요.
Mark: Now, we should go this way from here as he said.
자 이제 저 사람이 말한 대로 여기서 이 길로 가야 해.
Look! I can see the sign.
봐! 표지판이 보인다.
Julie: Right. But it says 200 meters. I think that's too far.
맞네, 200미터라고 쓰여 있는데.. 너무 먼 것 같아.
Mark: It's okay. We can enjoy the city street while walking.
괜찮아. 걸으면서 도시의 거리 구경을 하면 돼.
Julie: You're right. The map says we should turn right at the end of this street. And it goes to the park.
네 말이 맞아. 지도에는 길 끝에서 우회전 해야 한다고 나와 있네.
Mark: Oh, look! There are street musicians.
아 저 봐. 거리의 음악가들이야.
Julie: Wow, it's amazing.
와 멋지다.
Mark: They don't look like amateurs.
아마추어 같지 않은데.
Julie: Right. Their music is just great.
그러네. 음악이 훌륭한 걸.
Mark: Julie, I can see the bike rental shop here.
Julie, 여기 자전거 대여점이 있네.
Julie: Why don't we walk a little more?
좀더 걷는 게 어때?
Now I remember this area.
아! 이제 여기가 어딘지 기억난다.
If we turn right, there's another store. The rental price here is much cheaper.
우회전하면 가게가 하나 더 있어. 여기의 대여료가 훨씬 더 싸.
Mark: Okay. You mean that place over there?
오케이. 저기 있는 저 곳 말하는 거지?
Julie: There it is. 저기 있네.
It's perfect weather to ride a bike.
자전거 타기에는 완벽한 날씨야.
Mark: Yeah, I'm really expecting it. Let's go.
그래 정말 재미있겠다. 가자.

### Upgrade it!

Let's ride a bike.
자전거 타자.
Give me a ride.
절 좀 태워 주세요.
I need to take a break.
저는 휴식이 필요합니다.
Will you take a walk?
산책하겠습니까?
I'll take you to the market.
제가 당신을 데리고 시장에 가겠습니다.
The airport is nearby.
공항은 근처에 있다.
I can't find anything nearby.
근처에 아무것도 없다.
She has straight hair.

그녀는 직모다.
Go straight.
쭉 앞으로 가세요.
Keep it straight.
일직선을 유지하세요.
Don't move while sitting.
앉아 있을 때는 움직이지 마세요.
Will you feed my puppy while you are here?
여기 머무르는 동안 내 강아지에게 먹이를 좀 줄 수 있겠어?
I'll be away for a while.
잠깐 떠나있을 거다.
It's an amazing show.
그 공연은 멋지다.
What an amazing sky!
하늘이 정말 멋지다.
She is amazing.
그녀는 멋진 사람이다.
I want to make it perfect.
저는 완벽하게 하고 싶습니다.
He is a perfect man.
그는 완벽한 남자이다.
It's perfect!
그것은 완벽하다.
He's expecting you.
그가 당신을 기다리고 있습니다.
I expect to see you.
당신을 만나기를 기대합니다.
You make me expect something unusual in life.
당신은 나로 하여금 인생에서 특별한 무언가를 기대하고 만든다.

## Situation 16 Can you show me where I am?

### 제가 지금 어디에 있습니까?

Ann: Well, she said 100 meters from the post office, but··· Gee, it's not right.
그녀는 우체국에서 100미터 정도 더 가면 된다고 했는데. 에이 아닌데.
Excuse me. Can I ask you something?
실례합니다. 뭐 좀 물어봐도 되겠습니까?
Man: Sure. 네.
Ann: I'm lost. Can you help me?
길을 잃었어요. 도와주시겠어요?
Man: Sure, you're on the corner of Main Street and Park Avenue.
물론이지요. 당신은 지금 메인스트리트 와 파크 에비뉴가 만나는 지점에 있습니다.
Ann: Can you show me where I am on this map?
이 지도상에서 저의 위치를 말씀해주시겠어요?
Man: Okay. Let's see··· Now you are here at this point on the map.
네, 그러니까 지도 이 지점에 당신이 있군요.
Ann: I'm looking for the Central Theater.
저는 센트럴 극장을 찾고 있는데요.
Can you show me the way to the theater?
극장으로 가는 길을 가르쳐 주시겠어요?
Man: Um··· This way goes to Starry Park and I know it's just near here.
음.이 길로 가면 스타리 공원으로 이어지고, 이 근처란 건 알겠는데뭴
Ann: Yeah, I've heard it's somewhere around here.
네, 이 근처 어디란 것은 들었어요.
Man: Well, I don't know exactly. I'm not from around here myself, either.
정확하게 모르겠는데요.. 저도 이 지역 출신이 아니라서.
There's a police officer standing there. Why don't you ask him?
저기 경찰관이 있네요. 가서 물어보지 그래요?
Ann: OK. Thanks anyway. 네, 어쨌든 감사합니다.
Man: Bye. 안녕히 가십시오.
Ann: Excuse me, officer. 실례합니다. 경찰관님.
Officer: Yes, ma'am. 네.
Ann: I need some help. I'm going to the Central Theater.
도움이 필요합니다. 센트럴 극장에 가려고 합니다.
Is it this direction?
이 방향입니까?
Officer: Oh, it's right over there.
네 저기 바로 있네요.
You see the big signboard there?
저기 큰 간판이 보이지요?
Ann: Yes?
어디요?
Officer: That's the theater you're looking for.
저기가 당신이 찾고 있는 극장입니다.
Ann: Oh, it's very near! Thank you so much.
와 정말 가깝네요. 감사합니다.
Officer: My pleasure. 별말씀을요.

## Upgrade it!

Where's the Lost and Found?
분실물 센터가 어디 있습니까?
I'm lost!
나는 길을 잃었다.
She lost her baggage.
그녀는 가방을 잃었다.
It's somewhere around here.
이 근처 어딘가에 있다.
Are you going somewhere this summer?
이번 여름에 어디 가세요?
Tell me exactly what it is.
그게 뭔지 정확하게 얘기해라.
It's exactly the same.
정확히 똑같다.
I cannot answer exactly.
정확하게 대답할 수 없다.
Thanks anyway.
어쨌든 감사합니다.
Anyway, I'm not going.
어쨌든 나는 갈 거다.
I'm going this direction.
저는 이 쪽으로 갑니다.
Is this the direction you want?
이 방향으로 가고 싶으세요?
Let's ask for the directions.
길을 물어보자.
My pleasure. 천만에요.
It's a pleasure to help you.
당신을 돕게 되어서 기쁩니다.
Look at the map.
지도를 보세요.
Do you have the route map?
노선도 있으세요?
Let's buy a city map.
도시지도를 삽시다.
I don't know where I am on this map.
이 지도상에서 내 위치가 어딘지 모르겠어요.

# Unit 09 Health & Diet 건강과 다이어트

## Situation 17 I am on a diet.

### 저는 다이어트 중 이예요.

Brian: Hi Julie, Long time no see. How have you been?
안녕 Julie. 오랜만이구나. 어떻게 지냈니?

Julie : Hi, Brian! I have been busy because of my new project. 안녕 Brian. 새로 맡은 프로젝트가 있어서 계속 바빴어.

Brian: By the way, you look different but I am not quite sure what it is.
근데 너 달라 보인다, 하지만 정확하게 뭔지 모르겠어.

Julie : Well, I lost five kilos. I always wanted to lose these extra kilos.
5 킬로그램을 감량했어. 이 초과 체중을 항상 빼고 싶었어.

Brian: Wow, great! How did you do it? Were you on any special diet program? Let me guess, the Atkins Diet?
와 대단한걸. 어떻게 했어? 특별한 다이어트 방법이라도? 내가 맞춰볼게. 황제다이어트?

Julie : No, it is outdated now. I have been on a juice fasting program.
아니 그건 이미 한물갔어. 나는 주스 금식 다이어트를 했지.

Brian: I heard a lot of Hollywood stars love the program.
많은 할리우드 스타들이 그 방법을 좋아한다고 들었어.

Julie : Yeah, it is good for people who want to lose weight in a relatively short period of time.
그래. 비교적 단기간에 체중을 감량하려는 사람들에게 좋은 방법이야.

Brian: I am on a diet too. 나도 다이어트 중이야.

Julie : Really? But you look the same. How long? What kind? Did you lose some weight?
그래? 별차이가 없는데. 얼마나 되었니? 살은 좀 빠진 거니?

Brian: I just started it yesterday.
어제 막 시작했어.
I would call it a "one meal a day" diet.
일일 일식 다이어트 라고 나 할까.

Julie : Wow, you mean you only eat one meal a day?
어머나 세상에 하루에 한끼만 먹는다는 말이야?
How long are you going to do that?
얼마동안 할거야?

Brian: For about a month maybe.
한달 정도.
I only eat lunch.
점심만 먹어.
I really hate this extra fat, especially around my belly.
난 이 여분의 지방이 정말 싫어. 특히 배 주위의 살 말이야.

Julie : Well, I don't think it is good for your metabolism.
음 신진대사에 좋지 않을 것 같은데.
Some people even say that you should eat every three hours and five times a day to burn the calories more efficiently.
칼로리를 효율적으로 태우려면 매 세시간마다 하루 다섯 끼를 먹어야 한다고 말하는 사람들도 있어.

Brian: Really?
정말?
I think I have to visit an expert and ask for professional tips.
내 생각엔 전문가를 만나 전문적인 조언을 구해야 할 것 같아.

Julie : Please do that.
그렇게 해봐.
I can recommend someone for you.
내가 누군가를 추천해 줄 수 있어.
He is very popular and you have to arrange for a meeting at least two months ahead. I think he is fully booked now.
매우 인기 있는 사람이라 적어도 두 달 전에 예약을 해야 해. 지금은 예약이 꽉 찼을 걸.
Besides, soon it is bikini season and everyone is getting ready for it.
게다가 곧 비키니 시즌이라 모든 사람들이 비키니 입을 준비를 하고 있어.

Brian: Oh, he must make good money.
와! 돈을 정말 잘 벌겠네.

Julie : You can say that again! Here's his business card.
물론이지. 여기 그의 명함이 있어.
Call him right away!
당장 그에게 전화해 봐.

Brian: I will do that. Thanks. See you later.
그럴게. 고마워, 나중에 봐.

Julie : Bye, good luck! 안녕, 행운을 빌어.

## Upgrade it!

I hate you because I love you so much!
당신을 너무 사랑하기 때문에 증오한다.
Who do you hate?
당신은 누구를 증오하나요?
I don't hate anybody.
나는 누구도 싫어하지 않는다.
He is an expert on that matter.
그는 그 문제에 있어서는 전문가이다.
You should become an expert in at least one field.
너는 적어도 한 분야에 있어서는 전문가가 되어야 한다.
How long does it take to become a true expert?
진정한 전문가가 되려면 얼마나 걸립니까?
How many meals do you eat a day?
당신은 하루에 몇 끼를 먹습니까?
I make it a rule to have three square meals a day.
나는 하루에 세끼를 꼭 제대로 챙겨먹는다.
He has not eaten even one meal today.
그는 오늘 한끼도 먹지 못했다.
What do you recommend for my mother's birthday?
우리 어머니 생일 선물로 뭘 사주면 좋을 것 같니?
I recommend him as your assistant.
그를 당신의 조교로 추천합니다.
Why do you need some extra money?
왜 당신은 돈이 더 필요합니까?
I will pay extra if you do as I say.
내가 말하는 대로 하면 돈을 더 주겠다.
You should be extra careful with this one.
이것에 대해서는 특별히 조심해야 한다.
I only eat vegetables, not meat.
나는 고기는 먹지 않고 채소만 먹는다.
You are the only one for me.
내게는 당신뿐입니다.
The only way to get blessed is this.
축복을 받는 방법은 이것뿐입니다.
That style is outdated.
이 스타일은 유행이 지났다.
For some students, e-mail is already outdated.
일부 학생들에게 있어서 이메일은 이미 시대에 뒤처진 것이다.

It's an outdated expression.
그것은 진부한 표현이다.
He is popular among girls.
그는 여학생들 사이에 인기가 있다.
Who is the most popular in this class?
이 학급에서 가장 유명한 사람은 누구입니까?
The novel is not popular any longer.
그 소설은 더 이상 유명하지 않다.
How many times do you pray a day?
당신은 하루에 몇 차례나 기도를 합니까?
How many times do you eat a day?
하루에 몇 번 식사를 합니까?
I eat three times a day.
저는 하루에 세 번 식사를 합니다.
He is far ahead of me.
그는 나보다 많이 앞서있다.
My parents are ahead of the times.
나의 부모님들은 시대를 앞서 가신다.
Who is ahead of you in line?
줄에서 당신 앞에 누가 서 있습니까?
I need to lose weight.
나는 살을 빼야 한다.
How much weight did you lose last month?
지난 달 몇 킬로를 감량하였습니까?
He needs to gain some weight.
그는 체중을 좀 늘여야 한다.

## Situation 18 My father's so demanding!

### 저의 아버지는 너무

Julie : Hi Brian! Did you call the guy I recommended to you the other day?
안녕, Brian! 요전 날 내가 추천한 그 사람에게 전화해봤어?

Brian: No, I couldn't. I've been really busy because of my father.
아니 못했어. 아버지 때문에 정말 바빴거든.

Julie : What's up with your father?
아버지께 무슨 일이라도 생겼니?

Brian: He sprained his ankle while he was tending the garden. 정원손질 하시다가 발목을 삐셨어.

Julie : Oh, no! Is he okay now?
어머나 저런. 지금 괜찮으시니?

Brian: He is getting better and better every day.
매일 조금씩 나아지고 계셔.
But I have to be by his side all the time doing errands for him.
하지만 내가 아버지 심부름 하느라 항상 옆에 있어야만 해.
I am even tending the garden myself in the sun while he is ordering me what to do!
심지어는 아버지가 내게 명령 내리시고 나는 그에 따라 뙤약볕 속에서 직접 정원손질까지 하고 있다니까.
And he is so demanding and never satisfied with my work.
근데 우리 아버지는 너무 까다로우셔서 결코 내가 하는 일에 만족하시지 않아.

Julie : That must be a lot of work. 일이 정말 많겠구나.

Brian: You wouldn't believe it if you saw it with your own eyes.
직접 눈으로 보면 믿을 수 없을걸.
I have no personal life now. I mean, not at all.
난 사생활이 없어. 하나도 없다고.
I have to move my body all day long. What a life!
하루 종일 몸을 움직여야 한다니까. 정말 힘들어.

Julie : There is no use complaining about it.
거기에 대해서 불평해도 소용없어.
Try to look at the positive side.
긍정적인 면을 보려고 노력해 봐.

Brian: What do you mean? What is positive about it?
무슨 말이야? 긍정적으로 볼게 뭐가 있니?

Julie : You are helping your father and exercising at the same time.
넌 아버지를 돕고 동시에 운동도 하잖아.
Some people spend huge money just to get some exercise.
단지 운동만을 위해서 엄청 돈을 많이 쓰는 사람들도 있는데.

Brian: That's different! They are exercising and relaxing but I'm working. And it gives me stress.
그건 다르지. 그 사람들은 운동하며 휴식을 가지는 거고 나는 일하는 것이라 스트레스를 받거든.

Julie : You don't have to separate work from exercise.
일과 운동을 분리할 필요는 없잖아.
I heard on the radio that Australians' most preferred job is being a carpenter.
라디오에서 들었는데 호주에서 가장 인기 있는 직업이 목수래.
They think carpentry makes you exercise and

earn money at the same time.
호주인들은 목수일을 하면 운동도 하고 동시에 돈도 벌 수 있다고 생각해.

Brian: Killing two birds with one stone?
일석이조라고?
That makes sense!
그거 말 된다.
But still, it makes me crazy living for my father around the clock.
하지만 여전히 24시간 내내 아버지를 위해 산다는 건 정말 괴로운 일이야.
I know I am supposed to be more than willing to help my sick father. But I need my freedom.
아픈 아버지를 위해서 보다 기꺼이 도와드려야 한다는 것은 알지만 나도 자유가 필요해.

Julie : I understand. Have some patience. It won't last forever.
나도 이해해. 좀 참아. 영원히 그래야 할 건 아니니까.

Brian: Yeah, you are right. I am not a good son to complain about such a thing. I think I should repent.
그래, 네 말이 맞아. 그런 것에 대해 불평하다니 난 좋은 아들이 아니야. 뉘우쳐야 되겠어.

Julie : Come on. Don't blame yourself. Everyone would feel the same in your shoes. God will understand.
자책하지마. 누구라도 너의 상황이 되면 똑같이 느낄 거야. 하나님은 이해하실 걸.

Brian: Well, I am not so sure, though. 음 하지만 잘 모르겠어.

## Upgrade it!

I sprained my wrist while playing basketball.
농구하다가 팔목을 삐었다. .
He sprained his ankle while playing soccer.
그는 축구를 하다가 발목을 삐었다.
A sprained ankle is a very common injury.
발목을 삐는 것은 흔히 있는 부상이다.

They are tending to sick children in India.
그들은 인도에서 아픈 아이들을 돌보고 있다.
My father tends the garden as a hobby.
아버지는 취미로 정원을 돌보신다.

Korean boys tend to be more aggressive than Japanese ones. 한국 소년들은 일본의 소년들보다 더 적극적이다.

Your English is getting better every day.
당신의 영어가 매일 나아지고 있어요.
I am getting better at English.
나의 영어 실력이 점점 더 나아지고 있다.
You had better get used to it.
그것에 익숙해지는 게 좋을 거야.

I need a personal life. 나는 개인 생활이 필요하다.
That is personal information. I won't give it to you.
이건 사적인 정보이다. 너에게 밝히지 않을 거야.
Don't take it personally.
그것을 개인적으로 받아들이지 마세요. 당신에게 하는 말이라고 생각지 마세요.

You always complain about something.
너는 항상 무언가에 대해 불평한다.
Complaining does not help at all.
불평하는 것은 전혀 도움이 되지 않는다.
Why don't you stop complaining now?
이제 그만 불평하지 그래요?

Be positive! 긍정적으로 생각하시오.
Get a positive view of life!
인생에 대해서 긍정적인 시각을 가지시오.
Positive people tend to be more successful.
긍정적인 사람이 성공하는 경우가 더 많다.

They look the same. 그들은 똑 같아 보인다.
The results are the same as before.
결과가 지난 번과 똑같다.
The same thing happened to me last night.
같은 일이 어젯밤 내게 일어났다.

How much money do you spend a month?
한 달에 돈을 얼마나 쓰세요?
How would you like to spend the remaining time?
남은 시간을 어떻게 보내고 싶으세요?
You have to be very careful with the money you spend.
돈을 신중하게 소비해야 한다.
I spent the whole weekend doing homework.
주말 내내 숙제만 했다.

They are separated now. 그들은 지금 별거 중이다.
Separation is painful. 이별은 고통스럽다.

A fence separates the two gardens.
울타리가 있어서 두 개의 정원을 분리시키고 있다.
Do you really mean it? 진담이세요?
I mean it. 진담입니다.
What do you mean by that? 그게 무슨 뜻입니까?

Jesus Christ was a carpenter. 예수님은 목수였다.
To be a carpenter, you need special skills.
목수가 되기 위해서는 특별한 기술이 필요하다.
Is there anyone who wants to be a carpenter here?
여기 목수가 되고 싶은 사람이 있습니까?

## Unit 10 Events 이벤트

### Situation 19 My parents' wedding anniversary is coming up!
부모님의 결혼기념일이 다가오고 있어요.

Laura : Are you free this afternoon?
오늘 오후 시간 있니?

Julie : Well, I have no special plans yet. Why do you ask?
아직 특별한 약속은 없는데 왜 묻지?

Laura : I really want you to do me a favor.
꼭 내 부탁을 들어줬음 해.

Julie : What do you want from me?
내게 원하는 게 뭐지?

Laura : Come with me to the department store.
나랑 같이 백화점에 가자.

Julie : You mean, you want some help with shopping?
쇼핑하는 것 도와달라고?

Laura : Yeah, exactly! My parents' wedding anniversary is coming up. Actually it's next Monday!
바로 그거야. 부모님의 결혼기념일이 다가와서. 사실은 다음주 월요일이라니까.
It will be easier if you help me select the presents.
네가 선물 고르는 것을 도와주면 좀 더 수월할 거야.

Julie : Great! So what are you thinking of buying for them?
좋았어. 너는 뭘 사드리려고 생각하고 있니?

Laura : A scarf for my mom and a tie for my dad. What do you think?
엄마에게는 스카프를 아빠께는 넥타이를 사드리려고 하는데 너 생각은 어때?

Julie : Good! I bought the same things for my parents' wedding anniversary last month.
좋지. 지난 달 우리 부모님 결혼식에도 같은 걸 사드렸어.
Let's get moving. I have only three hours.
움직이자. 세 시간 밖에 없어.
I don't want to miss the 7:30 show. It's my favorite.
7시30분 프로를 놓치고 싶지 않아 좋아하거든.

Laura : Sure, It won't take long.
걱정 마, 오래 걸리진 않을 테니.
We can enjoy the show together at my house after shopping.
쇼핑 끝나고 우리 집에서 같이 보면 되겠다.
Let's order some Chinese food and enjoy it with the show.
중국음식을 주문해서 먹으면서 쇼를 재미있게 보자.

Julie : That's perfect! 그거 좋겠네.
You know I love Chinese food. I haven't had it for almost a month because my mom hates it.
내가 중국음식을 좋아하는데 우리 엄마가 싫어해서 거의 한달 동안 먹지를 못했어.

Laura : My parents are not coming home until after the show. 쇼가 끝날 때까지 부모님은 집에 오시지 않을 거야.
We have plenty of time to enjoy ourselves.
그러니 우리가 재미있게 놀 시간은 충분하지.

Julie : I'm so glad to have a friend like you.
너와 같은 친구를 두어서 정말 기뻐.
My mother never allows me to eat while watching TV.
우리 엄마는 TV보면서 절대 뭘 먹지 못하게 한다니까.

### Upgrade it!

I am free from 10 to 11 this morning.
오늘 아침10시부터 11시까지 시간이 있습니다.
Are you free tomorrow? 내일 시간이 있습니까?
If you were free now, what would you do?
지금 만약 시간이 있다면 뭘 하시겠어요?
Will you do me a favor?

내 부탁을 들어주겠어?
Do me a favor, please!
제발 내 부탁 좀 들어 줘!
Can I ask you a favor?
부탁을 하나 해도 되겠습니까?
I will miss the class because I have to go to the hospital.
병원에 가야 하기 때문에 수업에 가지 못하겠습니다.
Will you miss me after I am gone?
내가 떠나면 넌 내가 보고 싶을까?
The cat is missing. 고양이가 없어졌다.
What is your favorite drink?
좋아하는 음료수는 무엇입니까?
My favorite movie star is Jang Dong-gun.
내가 좋아하는 영화배우는 장동건입니다.
Math is my favorite.
수학은 내가 좋아하는 과목입니다.
You are not allowed to sit here.
당신은 여기 앉으면 안됩니다.
My mother does not allow me to go shopping alone.
저의 어머니는 내가 혼자 쇼핑 가는 것을 허락하지 않습니다.
Would you allow me to go home now?
이제 집에 가는 것을 허락하시겠어요?
Do you have any special plans for tomorrow?
내일 특별한 약속 있습니까?
You are so special!
당신은 정말 특별한 사람입니다.
Is he someone special to you?
그는 당신에게 특별한 존재입니까?
Let's order some food. I am hungry.
음식을 좀 주문하자. 배가 고프다.
What would you order for me?
날 위해 뭘 주문해 주겠니?
Anybody who ordered pepperoni pizza here?
여기 페퍼로니 피자 주문하신 분?
We have plenty of time before the class starts.
수업이 시작되기 전까지 시간 많이 남아 있다.
He has plenty of money.
그는 돈이 많다.
Money is never too plenty.
돈이 아무리 많아도 지나치지 않다.
It will take about two hours.
두 시간 정도 소요될 것이다.
It took only half an hour to complete the assignment.
그 과제를 완성하는데 거의 삼십 분이 걸렸다.
Take it or leave it.
하든지 말든지 결정하시오.
Did you enjoy the party last night?
지난 밤 파티 재미있었나요?
Let's enjoy ourselves at the picnic.
소풍 가서 재미있게 놀자.
He is so perfect for me.
그는 내게 딱 맞는 남자다.
You can't be perfect in everything.
모든 것을 다 잘할 수 는 없다.
There is no perfect solution for the problem.
그 문제에 대한 완벽한 해결책은 없다.

## Situation 20 I'm getting engaged!

### 나 약혼할거야.

Laura : Hello, this is Laura speaking. Can I speak to Julie please?
여보세요 저는 Laura라고 하는데요 Julie와 통화할 수 있을까요?

Julie : Hi, Laura! This is me, Julie.
안녕 Laura. 나 Julie야.

Laura : I thought it was your mother.
난 네 엄마인 줄 알았어.
I always have a problem recognizing your voice.
언제나 너의 목소리를 구별하지 못한다니까.
You and your mother sound the same.
너와 너의 엄마가 목소리가 똑같아.

Julie : Is that so? Everyone who calls my house says the same. What's up?
그러니? 우리집에 전화하는 사람들은 다 그렇게 이야기 하더라. 무슨 일이야?

Laura : Oh, something big is up. You won't believe it. I am getting engaged!
큰 일이 있어. 넌 믿지 못할 거야. 나 약혼할거다.

Julie : What? Oh my God! You mean you are getting engaged to Mark?
뭐라고? 어머나 세상에! Mark랑 약혼할 거라고?
Or is there another guy? 아니면 다른 남자랑?

Laura : Come on! Mark is the only guy for me.
이거 왜 이러니. 내게는 Mark가 유일한 남자야.
You know how crazy I am about Mark.
내가 Mark를 얼마나 좋아하는지 너도 알잖아.
I am the fiance of Mark. *MY* Mark! I am so excited!

난 Mark의 약혼녀라고 나의 Mark야. 참 신난다.

Julie : You should be. Tell me about the details.
당연 그렇겠지. 자세하게 이야기 해 봐.
Did he ask you to marry him? Or was it the other way around?
그가 너에게 청혼했니 아니면 그 반대니?

Laura : Of course it was him asking me to marry him.
물론 그가 내게 청혼을 했지.
You know how long I have waited for this to happen.
이런 일이 있기를 얼마나 내가 기다려 왔는지.
After six years, he finally proposed to me.
6년이 지나고야 비로소 그가 내게 청혼을 한 거야.

Julie : When did it happen? And where?
언제 그랬어? 장소는?

Laura : An hour ago in the park near my house.
한 시간 전에 우리 집 근처 공원에서.
We were sitting on the bench and he suddenly took out roses from his bag and kneeled down in front of me, asking, "Will you marry me?"
벤치에 앉아 있는데 그가 갑자기 장미를 가방에서 꺼내더니 내 앞에 무릎을 꿇고 물어보는 거야. 나랑 결혼해 주겠어?
Isn't it so romantic?
너무 낭만적이지 않아?

Julie : Wow, it is not like him.
어머나 평소의 그답지 않네.
I always thought that he is kind of unromantic and cool-headed.
그는 좀 낭만과는 거리가 멀고 냉철한 사람이라고 항상 생각했는데.

Laura : I thought the same.
나도 그렇게 생각했었어.
I still can't believe it.
아직도 믿을 수 없다니까.
You will never imagine how many times I pinched my arm to see if it was real.
사실인지 확인하려고 몇 번이나 나의 팔을 꼬집었는지 넌 상상도 못할 거야.
We are going to have a small engagement party this weekend.
이번 주말에 조촐한 약혼식을 하려고 해.
And we are going to get married as soon as he finishes his military service.
그리고 그가 군복무를 마치자 마자 결혼할거야.

Julie : I am so envious of you guys. Am I invited? And who else are you going to invite?
너희들 정말 부럽다. 나도 초대할 거지? 그리고 또 누굴 초대할 건데?

Laura : We are inviting about ten people including you.
널 포함해서 약 열 명 정도 초대하려고 해.
It is really a small party just among very close friends.
친한 친구들끼리만 모여서 조촐하게 할거야.

## Upgrade it!

You sound sick.
너 목소리를 들어보니 아픈 것 같은데.
Do I sound okay?
내 목소리 괜찮니? 내가 한말 괜찮은 것 같아?
Does it sound okay to you?
네가 듣기엔 괜찮은 것 같니?
I got engaged to your father when I was only 20.
너의 아버지와 약혼 했을 때에는 불과 20세 밖에 안되었다.
This is my engagement ring.
이것은 내 약혼반지야.
I am engaged to Mark.
나는 Mark와 약혼한 사이야.
How many people are you inviting to the party?
파티에 몇 명이나 초대할 겁니까?
Is he invited to your birthday party?
그도 너의 생일파티에 초대했니?
He invited me to his house.
그는 나를 그의 집에 초대했다.
I forgave him because he kneeled and asked for mercy.
그가 무릎을 꿇고 용서를 구했기 때문에 나는 그를 용서했다.
Do not kneel on the floor. It's very dirty.
바닥에 무릎 꿇고 앉지 마라. 대단히 더럽다.
Let's kneel and pray to God.
무릎을 꿇고 하나님께 기도합시다.
It's all five of us including you.
널 포함해서 총 5명이다.
The meal includes coffee and dessert.
식사에는 커피와 디저트가 포함되어 있습니다.
The cost does not include the airfare.
비용에는 항공료가 포함되어 있지 않습니다.
Are you married or not?
당신은 기혼입니까 미혼입니까?

How old were you when you got married?
당신은 결혼할 때 몇 살이었나요?
I am married to an American citizen.
저는 미국 시민권자와 결혼했습니다.
The accident happened two hours ago.
사고는 두 시간 전에 일어났다.
It can happen to anybody.
그런 일은 누구에게나 일어날 수 있다.
I happened to see your boyfriend on the way home.
집으로 가는 도중에 우연히 너의 남자친구를 보았다.
Suddenly it came to my mind.
갑자기 그런 생각이 들었다.
He suddenly appeared out of nowhere.
그는 갑자기 어딘가에서 나타났다.
Suddenly, he burst into laughter.
그는 갑자기 웃음을 터뜨렸다.
I am envious of you. 나는 당신이 부럽다.
Everyone is envious of his talents.
모든 사람들이 그의 재능을 부러워한다.
I am not envious of anybody. I am content as I am now.
나는 누구도 시기하지 않는다. 현재 나의 모습에 만족한다.
I pinched my thigh to stay awake.
잠들지 않으려고 허벅지를 꼬집었다.
The shoes pinch me at the heels.
그 신발은 뒤꿈치가 꽉 낀다.
Pinch me on my hand. 내 손을 꼬집어 줘.
You can never imagine what happened.
무슨 일이 있었는지 너는 상상할 수 없을 거야.
You are free to imagine there is no hell but it exists.
지옥이 없다고 상상하는 것은 너의 자유다 하지만 지옥은 실제로 있다.
Just imagine how happy I was!
내가 얼마나 행복했을지 상상 좀 해봐!

## Unit 11 Trouble 문제

### Situation 21 I had a fight with my boyfriend!

### 남자친구와 싸웠어.

Laura : Julie, you look terrible! Is anything wrong?
Julie, 안색이 좋지 않네 뭐 좋지 않은 일이라도 있니?
Julie : Yeah, I had a fight with my boyfriend.
응 남자친구랑 싸웠어.
Laura : That's too bad. Was it serious? Who started it?
저런. 심하게 싸웠니? 싸움을 누가 시작했어?
Julie : Well, listen. This is what happened. I was preparing for my test in the library and Tommy came over and asked me to go out for dinner.
한번 들어봐. 일이 이렇게 된 거야. 내가 도서관에서 시험 준비를 하고 있었는데 Tommy가 다가 와서 저녁을 먹으러 가자는 거야.
But it was only five o'clock and I did not want to get interrupted for another hour.
근데 다섯 시 밖에 되지 않았고 한 시간 정도는 더 방해 받지 않고 공부하고 싶었어.
Laura: So you said no, right?
그래서 안 간다고 했구나 그지?
Julie : Yes, and I asked him to come back an hour later.
응 그리고 내가 그에게 한 시간 후 다시 오라고 말했어.
And he suddenly got angry and yelled at me.
그런데 그가 갑자기 화를 내더니 나에게 소리를 치는 거야.
Laura: You mean in the library?
도서관 안에서 말이야?
Julie : Yeah, there were a lot of people and I was so embarrassed.
응, 사람들이 많이 있어서 정말 당황했다니까.
I don't want to see him again.
나는 다시는 그를 보고 싶지 않아.
Laura : How did you respond?
그래서 넌 어떻게 했니?
Julie : I just packed my things and hurried out.
그냥 내 물건들을 싸서 황급히 나왔지 뭐.
He tried to follow me but I didn't even look at his face and ran away.
그가 날 따라 오려고 했지만 그의 얼굴도 보기 싫어서 도망쳤어.
Laura : Did he call? 그가 전화했니?
Julie : Yeah, several times. But I didn't want to talk to him.
응, 몇 번 했어. 근데 난 그와 얘기하고 싶지 않았어.
Laura : So, what are you going to do now?
그래서 이제 어떻게 할건데?
Julie : I am going to break up with him.
그와 헤어질 거야.
I can never understand a man yelling in public places, no matter what! What do you think?

난 공공장소에서 고함치는 남자는 절대로 이해할 수 없어 무슨 이유라도 용납할 수 없어.

Laura : I totally agree with you.
나도 너와 같은 생각이야.
But he has been so well-mannered and I don't understand why he did that.
근데 그는 참 매너도 좋은 남자였는데 왜 그런 행동을 했는지 이해되지 않아.
Is he going through some personal crises?
그가 개인적으로 힘든 일을 겪고 있나?

Julie : I don't want to even think about it.
그 생각은 하기도 싫어.
You know how it feels to get scowled at by all the students in the library. It was so horrible.
도서관에 있는 모든 학생들이 자신을 노려볼 때의 그 기분 너도 알잖아. 끔찍했다고.

Laura : Calm down and go see a movie or something for a change.
진정하고 기분전환을 위해 영화를 보든지 해.

Julie : I want to, but I can't. I have to study.
그러고 싶은데 그럴 수가 없어. 공부해야 하거든.

Laura : That's too bad. Is there anything I can do for you? 저런. 내가 해 줄 수 있는 게 있을까?
Will you feel better if I buy you a nice dinner?
근사한 저녁식사를 내가 사주면 기분이 나아질 것 같니?

Julie : You are so sweet, but I don't think I can eat any food right now.
넌 참 친절하구나. 근데 지금은 아무것도 먹을 수 없을 것 같아.
I am so upset.
정말 기분이 좋지 않아.

## Upgrade it!

That's so sweet of you.
당신은 참 친절하시군요.
The coffee's so sweet. How many spoonfuls of sugar did you put in it?
커피가 참 달다. 설탕 몇 스푼 넣었니?
If you eat too many sweets, you will have cavities.
단 것을 너무 많이 먹으면 충치가 생길 것이다.
I am so upset because you rejected my offer.
네가 나의 제안을 거절해서 너무 속상하다.
I have an upset stomach. 속이 거북하다.
If you feel upset, try to cheer up by listening to music.
기분이 언짢으면 음악을 들어서 기분을 밝게 해.
You look terrible today. Are you sick or something?
오늘 좋아 보이지 않네. 어딘가 아픈 거니?
The weather is terrible.
날씨가 엉망이다.
He is a terrible person.
그는 비열한 사람이다.
I don't want to get interrupted in the middle of doing something.
나는 뭔가를 한참 하는 도중에 방해 받고 싶지 않다.
He interrupted our conversation.
그는 우리의 대화를 방해했다.
Who is making this noise?
누가 이렇게 시끄럽게 하나?
The creaking sound interrupts the class!
삐걱거리는 소리 때문에 수업에 방해가 된다.
I was embarrassed when he called out my name loudly on the street.
그가 내 이름을 길거리에서 크게 불렀을 때 정말 당황했다.
It's embarrassing to watch a couple kissing in public places.
공공장소에서 커플이 키스하는 것을 보게 되면 당황스럽다.
What was the most embarrassing moment in your life?
당신의 생애에서 가장 당황한 순간은 언제였나요?
I broke up with my boyfriend.
나는 내 남자친구와 헤어졌다.
I am thinking of breaking up with my boyfriend.
나는 내 남자친구와 헤어질까 생각 중이다.
I'm interested in breaking things up.
나는 물건들을 분해하는 것을 좋아한다.
Stop yelling. The baby is sleeping now.
그만 소리질러. 아기가 지금 자고 있다.
My mom was so furious and started to yell at me.
엄마가 너무 화나서 나에게 소리치기 시작했다.
Well-mannered men never yell.
매너 있는 남자들은 절대로 고함치지 않는다.
I stepped on his foot and he scowled at me.
나는 그의 발을 밟았다. 그러자 그가 나를 노려보았다.
I saw his scowling face in my dream.
나는 그의 화난 얼굴을 내 꿈속에서 보았다.
I smiled at his scowling face.
그가 화난 얼굴을 보고 나는 미소를 지어 주었다.
He is ill-mannered.
그는 매너가 나쁘다.

There are so many ill-mannered people.
매너가 나쁜 사람들이 너무 많다.
Don't you know any manners?
넌 매너도 모르니?
Let's hurry. 서두릅시다.
We are in such a hurry. 우리는 지금 급하다.
I hurried into the house.
나는 서둘러서 집으로 들어갔다.

## Situation 22 I have to clean up the house!

## 나는 집을 청소해야 한다.

Laura : Hello, Laura speaking.
여보세요. Laura입니다.

Julie : Hi, Laura. 안녕, Laura.
This is Julie and I want to ask you a favor and please don't say no.
나 Julie야. 너에게 부탁을 하나 하고 싶은데 꼭 들어줘.

Laura : Oh, are you in trouble? 뭐 사고라도 친 거니?

Julie : Yes, and it is huge. I don't know what to do about it. 응 크게 쳤어. 어떻게 해야 할 지 모르겠어.
You are the only person who can save me from this.
나를 구해 줄 수 있는 사람은 너뿐이야.

Laura : What happened, you trouble maker?
무슨 일인데 이 말썽꾸러기!

Julie : My parents went on vacation, you know.
너도 알다시피 우리 부모님이 휴가 가셨잖아.

Laura : Yeah, to celebrate their 25th wedding anniversary.
그렇지 25주년 결혼기념일 축하하러 가셨지.
They went to France, right?
프랑스로 가신 것 맞지?

Julie : Yeah, and they were not supposed to come home until next week.
응 담 주 까진 집에 돌아오시지 않을 예정이었거든.
And I had a party with my other friends last night.
그래서 어젯밤 다른 친구들과 파티를 했지 뭐야.
I thought of inviting you but you had this big exam coming up.
너를 초대할까 생각도 했는데 넌 큰 시험을 앞두고 있어서.
So I didn't even tell you about it because I was kind of sorry.
그래서 미안해서 파티 얘기도 너에게는 하지 않았어.

Laura : You had a party last night at your parents' house?
어젯밤 너희 부모님 댁에서 파티를 했다고?
Are you insane? Your parents will kill you if they find out about it.
너 제정신이니? 그 사실을 알게 되면 네 부모님들이 널 가만두지 않을 걸.

Julie : I know and I got the phone call from my father just now.
나도 알아. 근데 방금 아버지 전화를 받았어.

Laura : What did he say? 뭐라고 하셨는데?

Julie : He said they are arriving home in two hours.
두 시간 후에 집에 도착하신다는 거야.
He had to cancel the remaining itinerary because of an important meeting.
중요한 미팅 때문에 나머지 일정을 취소해야만 했대.

Laura : Wow, so what do you want from me?
어머나. 그래서 내가 뭘 해주길 바라니?

Julie : The house is a mess because I just woke up to answer my father's phone call.
아버지의 전화를 받느라 방금 일어났기 때문에 집이 엉망이야.
I can never clean it up myself within two hours.
혼자서는 도저히 두 시간 내에 청소할 수 없다니까.

Laura : Okay, you need me to clean up the place.
알았어. 집 청소를 해달라는 거지.
I will hurry to your house though I am doing something important now. I don't want to get you killed by your parents.
지금 중요한 일을 하던 중이지만 서둘러서 너의 집으로 가지. 너의 부모님이 널 죽이는 걸 원치 않으니까.

Julie : I am so happy to have a friend like you. Thanks a million.
너와 같은 친구를 두어서 정말 기뻐. 대단히 고마워.

## Upgrade it!

I am in trouble. Please help me.
문제가 생겼어. 도와줘.

I have trouble reading the book. The letters are too small.
그 책을 잘 못 읽겠어. 글자가 너무 작아.
Someone will be there for you when you are in trouble.
너에게 문제가 생기면 누군가가 도와 줄 거야.
Let's cancel the original plan.
원래의 계획을 취소합시다.
We cancelled the party.
우리는 파티를 취소했다.
Why did they cancel the order?
왜 그들은 주문을 취소했나요?
The living room is in such a mess.
거실이 엉망진창이다.
He can mess up your life. Break up with him.
그는 너의 삶을 망칠 수 있다. 그와 헤어져.
The room is messy. 그 방은 어질러져 있다.
I am not hungry because I had a huge breakfast.
나는 배고프지 않다. 아침을 거하게 먹었거든.
He made a huge mistake.
그는 엄청난 실수를 했다.
My boyfriend and I had a huge fight last night.
남자친구와 난 어젯밤 크게 싸웠다.
You saved my life.
당신은 내 생명을 구해주었습니다.
Let's save it for later use.
그건 나중에 쓰기 위해 보관해 둡시다.
I saved my face thanks to you.
당신 덕택에 제 체면을 유지했습니다.
When is your wedding anniversary?
당신의 결혼 기념일이 언제입니까?
Tomorrow is our 2nd anniversary.
내일은 우리의 2주년 기념일이다.
What is good as an anniversary present?
기념일 선물로 뭐가 좋아요?
I woke up late this morning?
오늘 아침 제가 늦게 일어났나요?
Wake him up. It's time to go to school.
그를 깨우세요. 학교 갈 시간입니다.
I want a wake-up call at 6:00 tomorrow.
내일 6시에 모닝콜 부탁합니다.
What time are they arriving?
그들은 언제 도착합니까?
He arrived at two in the afternoon.
그는 오후 2시에 도착했다.
When I arrived home, it was almost midnight.
내가 집에 도착했을 때는 거의 자정이 되어 있었다.

What are you going to do during the remaining vacation? 남은 방학기간 동안 무엇을 할 예정입니까?
It remains to be seen whether he will keep his word.
그가 약속을 지킬지 어쩔지는 두고 볼 일이다.
I want to remain as your true friend.
나는 너의 진정한 친구로 남고 싶다.
A lot of people came to my house to celebrate my birthday.
많은 사람들이 나의 생일을 축하하기 위해서 우리 집에 왔다.
Let's celebrate our love. 우리의 사랑을 축하합시다.
I am holding a party to celebrate our reunion.
우리의 재결합을 축하하기 위해서 나는 파티를 할 겁니다.

## Unit 12 Future Plans 미래 계획

### Situation 23 I want to run my own business.

나는 내 사업을 하고 싶다.

Laura : What are you doing? 지금 뭐하고 있어?
Julie : You see I am studying.
공부하고 있는 거 안보이니?
Laura : What for? The mid term exam just ended. You need a break.
왜? 중간고사가 막 끝났는데. 휴식이 필요할 텐데.
Julie : No, I don't think so.
아니 내 생각은 달라.
I have to prepare for my future.
내 미래를 준비해야 해.
Laura : What exactly are you preparing for?
정확히 무슨 준비를 하는데?
Julie : I want to get a job right after graduation and I have to study very hard because of the cut-throat competition.
난 졸업하자마자 취직을 하고 싶어. 그래서 극심한 경쟁 때문에 굉장히 열심히 공부해야 해.
Laura: Well, entering a company is not the only way.
글쎄 취직하는 것만이 방법은 아니잖아.
Today the weather's just too beautiful to stay indoors.
오늘 실내에 있기에는 날씨가 너무 좋다.
Let's get outside and plan our bright future together in the sun.
밖으로 나가자 그리고 햇살 속에서 우리의 밝은 미래를 계획해 보자.

Julie : You are so carefree.
넌 정말 태평이구나.
What are you going to do after graduation if you can't pass the company entrance examination?
입사시험에 붙지 못하면 졸업 후 어떻게 하려고 해? You know it's hard. 시험이 어려운 건 알지?

Laura: Yeah, actually it's too hard for me and I gave it up all gdy.
응, 사실 내게는 너무 심하게 어려워서 난 이미 포기했어.

Julie : What are you talking about? My mother would kill me if I couldn't get a job after graduation.
무슨 말이야? 내가 졸업 후 취직을 못하면 우리 엄마는 날 가만 두지 않을 걸.

Laura : I am going to run my own business.
난 내 사업을 할 거야.
If you are interested I can show you some of my business plans.
너도 관심이 있으면 내 사업계획서를 좀 보여주지.
They are not complete yet, but it will be very intriguing.
아직 완성된 것은 아니지만 분명히 흥미로울 거야.

Julie : Really? Why didn't you tell me anything about them yet?
정말? 왜 진작 얘기하지 않았어?
Of course I am interested. Tell me about it.
당연히 관심이 있지. 내게 이야기 해봐.

Laura : I am not going to tell you here in this stuffy library.
여기 숨 막히는 도서관 속에서는 얘기 안 할 거야.
Pack your bags and follow me outdoors. After you hear, you will probably beg me to include you in my future business.
책 싸서 날 따라 밖으로 나와. 내 말을 듣고 나면 아마도 내 미래 사업에 너도 참여 시켜 달라고 매달릴걸.

Julie : What makes you so confident?
넌 왜 그리 자신만만하니?

Laura : Well, you will see when you hear my plans. Let's go!
듣고 나면 알게 될 거야. 가자.

Julie : Okay, It won't hurt. Anyway, I have nothing to lose.
좋았어. 나쁠 건 없겠지. 내가 손해 볼 건 없으니까.

Laura : Nothing to lose? Come on, trust me. You have everything to gain.
손해 볼 게 없다고? 이거 봐 내 말을 믿어. 무조건 얻는 거라니까.

## Upgrade it!

I am confident that I will win the race.
나는 경주에 이길 자신이 있다.
Be confident. 자신감을 가지세요.
You are overly confident.
당신은 자신감이 너무 지나쳐요.
After graduation, I will enter a company.
졸업 후 나는 회사에 취직할 거다.
What are you going to do after graduation?
졸업 후 뭘 하거니?
When is the graduation ceremony?
졸업식이 언제입니까?
Give me a break! 좀 봐주라.
We'll have a coffee break for thirty minutes.
우리는 삼십 분 동안 커피휴식을 가질 것이다.
Let's have a cigarette break for ten minutes and continue.
십분 동안 담배휴식을 가지고 계속하자.
The room is stuffy. Open the window.
이 방이 답답하다. 창문을 열어라.
Isn't it stuffy in here? 이 안이 답답하지 않니?
I have a stuffy nose because of my cold.
나는 감기 때문에 코가 막혔다.
Competition is fierce these days.
요즘은 경쟁이 치열하다.
There was less competition in the past.
과거에는 경쟁이 덜 심했다.
I need some information on the competition.
그 경기에 대해서 정보가 필요하다.
I enjoy playing sports outdoors.
나는 야외 스포츠를 즐긴다.
Let's enjoy the weather outdoors.
밖에 나가서 날씨를 즐기자.
Where is the entrance gate?
입구가 어디입니까?
When is the college entrance examination?
대학입학시험이 언제 입니까?
Entrance is free. 입장은 무료입니다.
That's not my job.
그것은 내가 할 일이 아니다.
What kind of job would you like to have?

요즈음 어떤 일을 하고 싶니?
I've got a new job.
나는 새 직장을 구했다.
Do you trust me?
당신은 나를 신뢰합니까?
Trust me.
나를 믿어라.
We need some time to build trust between ourselves.
우리 사이에 신뢰를 쌓기 위해서는 시간이 좀 필요하다.
I need to gain some weight.
살이 좀 쪄야 한다.
Gain some points after you fill out the survey form.
설문조사를 작성하시고 포인트를 얻어가세요.
No pains, no gains.
노력함이 없으면 얻는 것도 없다.
Complete the mission please.
임무를 완수하세요.
My job is complete now.
이제 내 일을 다 완성했다.
It requires complete devotion.
그것은 완벽한 헌신을 필요로 한다.

## Situation 24 You are a promising young

### 당신은 유망한 젊은이

Professor : I saw your proposal for the final term paper. I liked that idea very much.
자네의 기말페이퍼 제안서를 봤다네. 아이디어가 좋던걸.

Kevin : Thank you, Dr. Holt.
감사합니다. Holt 박사님.

Professor : Where did you get the idea?
어디서 그런 발상을 얻었나?

Kevin : Actually I have been thinking of it for a long time.
사실은 오랫동안 생각해 오던 거예요.
I am going to open my own business based on the idea.
그 아이디어를 가지고 저의 사업을 할 거예요.

Professor : Oh, really? It means you thought about the details of the plan already?
오 정말? 그럼 이미 상세한 계획까지 세워 놓았단 말인가?

Kevin : Yes, and I have done much of the market research as well.
네, 그렇습니다. 시장조사도 꽤 해 놓았습니다.

Professor : Brilliant! I am very curious. Are you going to give me more detailed presentation of your plans?
대단하군. 궁금한걸. 상세하게 설명 좀 해 주겠나?

Kevin : Of course if you are interested.
관심이 있으시면 당연히 그러지요.
But now I have to hurry to my accounting class.
하지만 저는 지금 회계수업에 서둘러 가야 해요.

Professor : What about tomorrow at two? Meet me at my office.
내일 두시는 어떤가? 내 사무실에서 만나세.
There is a national contest for business plans and only college students are eligible. With a little help, you have a good chance of winning, I am sure.
사업계획서 전국대회가 있는데 대학생만 참가자격이 있어. 좀 도움을 받으면 자네가 우승할 승산이 있다네.

Kevin : Wow, I am excited. Tomorrow at two would be fine.
와 기대되네요. 내일 두 시 좋습니다.
As a matter of fact, I always wanted to discuss it with someone who has more knowledge and experience.
사실 지식과 경험이 풍부하신 누군가와 이 문제를 가지고 얘기를 항상 하고 싶었습니다.

Professor : Well then, see you tomorrow. Prepare some more documents to back up your ideas.
그렇다면 내일 보세. 아이디어를 뒷받침할 만한 자료를 좀 더 가지고 오게나.

Kevin : Don't worry about it, ma'am. I have lots of them. 걱정하지 마십시오. 자료는 많이 있습니다.

Professor : You are a promising young man.
자네는 유망한 젊은이일세.
You will surely make an excellent entrepreneur.
분명히 뛰어난 기업가가 되겠는걸.

Kevin : Do you really think so? Thank you, ma'am. I'm so flattered.
정말 그렇게 생각하세요? 감사합니다. 우쭐해지네요.
I will be all ready for tomorrow's presentation. I won't disappoint you.

내일 프레젠테이션 준비를 철저히 하겠습니다. 실망시켜 드리지 않을게요.

Professor : You've already proven yourself. Don't overwork yourself.
이미 자네의 능력을 증명했으니 너무 지나치게 열심히 하지는 말게나.
Let's discuss it together over tea and make some improvements.
차 마시면서 토론을 하고 좀 더 낫게 고쳐 보세나.

Kevin : All right, Dr. Holt. See you tomorrow and have a nice day.
좋습니다. Holt 박사님. 내일 뵙겠습니다. 좋은 하루 보내세요.

Professor : Bye. 잘 가게나.

## Upgrade it!

I opened the book.
나는 책을 펼쳤다.
The gate is open.
문이 열려 있다.
Open sesame!
열려라 참깨.
Aren't you curious about the results?
당신은 결과에 대해 궁금하지 않으세요?
She has always been the curious type.
그녀는 항상 호기심이 많은 스타일이었다.
Curiosity killed the cat.
호기심이 너무 지나치면 해롭다.
You will make a good husband.
당신은 좋은 남편이 되겠다.
You will make a good teacher.
당신은 좋은 교사가 되겠습니다.
He will make it.
그는 해낼 거야. 그는 올 수 있을 거야.
Let's discuss it over lunch.
점심 먹으면서 토론하자.
They discussed the matter at length.
그들은 그 문제에 대해서 장황하게 토론했다.
Let's discuss it later.
그 문제에 대해서 나중에 토의하자.
Are you disappointed?
당신은 실망했습니까?
Nothing disappoints me.
어떠한 것도 나를 실망시킬 수 없다.
Did I disappoint you?
내가 당신을 실망시켰나요?
Let's prepare for the interview.
인터뷰 준비를 합시다.
My mom is preparing lunch.
어머니께서 점심 준비를 하고 계시다.
Are you preparing for the test?
시험 준비를 하고 있습니까?
You flattered me.
당신이 칭찬해 주어 우쭐합니다.
I am so flattered.
정말 우쭐해지는 걸요.
It is very flattering.
기분 좋습니다.
Don't worry. Be happy.
걱정하지 말고 행복한 생각을 하세요.
I am worried about you.
나는 당신이 걱정됩니다.
I am not worried at all.
나는 전혀 걱정되지 않습니다.
You are an excellent student.
당신은 훌륭한 학생입니다.
The test results are excellent.
시험의 결과가 훌륭하다.
What is so excellent about his report?
이 보고서가 뭐가 그렇게 뛰어나?
Can you prove that you are loyal?
당신이 충성스럽다는 것을 어떻게 증명할 수 있지?
He proved himself to be faithful.
그는 자기가 충성스럽다는 것을 증명해 보였다.
Can you prove that God exists?
하나님께서 계시다는 것을 증명할 수 있어요?
Chances are slim. 가능성이 희박하다.
There is a good chance that you will win the game.
네가 경기에 이길 가능성이 크다.
I don't want to take any chances.
나는 어떠한 위험도 무릅쓰고 싶지 않다.